∞

Bless Me, Father,
for I Have Kids

Also from Sophia Institute Press®
by Susie Lloyd:

Please Don't Drink the Holy Water!

Susie Lloyd

Bless Me, Father, for I Have Kids

SOPHIA INSTITUTE PRESS®
Manchester, New Hampshire

Sophia Institute Press®
Box 5284, Manchester, NH 03108
1-800-888-9344
www.sophiainstitute.com

Library of Congress Cataloging-in-Publication Data

Lloyd, Susie, 1966-
  Bless me, Father, for I have kids / Susie Lloyd.
    p. cm.
  ISBN 978-1-933184-40-1 (pbk. : alk. paper) 1. Home
schooling — Humor. 2. Catholics — Humor. I. Title.
PN6231.H56L65 2009
814'.6 — dc22

                                                        2009003348

09 10 11 12 13 14   10 9 8 7 6 5 4 3 2 1

To the children,
who are frequently called expensive.
To us you are priceless.

∝

Contents

Familiarity Breeds

A Little Lower Than the Angels . . .
Okay, a *Lot* Lower

The Uninterrupted Life Is Not Worth Living

Get on Your Knees and
Thank the Lord You're on Your Feet

∞

∞

Bless Me, Father,
for I Have Kids

"Four, five, six, seven . . . Are all these kids yours? I feel sorry for ya!"

∞

Familiarity Breeds

∞

Unto Us a Son Is Born

Gender has been identified as male. I was sitting alone in my bedroom leafing through my prenatal records — just to see if I had any communicable diseases — when the words jumped off the page. They'd put it in **bold;** as if finding out I was carrying a boy after six girls wouldn't be quite staggering enough. My first reaction was to cry.

Images of a nameless, faceless son, adrift in a sea of estrogen, floated through my mind. Granted, this was probably due to a momentary surge of *hysterione* — the pregnancy hormone. You never know when to take it seriously.

The next thing I did was tell my husband. I was counting on him to talk me down. You see, Greg is not one of these sensitive males who are so in style these days. For instance, during a really poignant scene in a movie — say, when the hero reveals himself to the heroine as the man who has loved her all along although she didn't know it and he's finally just about to kiss her — Greg can be relied on to say, "Wow! He's a great actor!"

In our household of seven females, we have enough romance movies to keep any boy chronically ill. That's what worried me. How would a baby boy fit in?

What would he do with a drawerful of headless naked Barbies? Would the girls tie an apron on him and make him play house? Or make him stand in for the prince in their never-ending fairytale plays?

All this was what I wanted Greg to sort out for me. And more.

The "more" was the girls. You see, for years people had acted disappointed in our boyless family. During this last pregnancy, friends had been telling us to "think positively," and relatives gave us blue blankies. Strangers analyzed my egg shape and pronounced that this time we'd be "lucky."

With no clue about the news I'd just received, the girls handled this by declaring a pink crusade: proclaiming loud and clear to all and sundry who ventured to comment that *we wanted another girl.* Every day they primed the smallest soldier, our two-year-old, as if she were learning her catechism:

"Melanie — do you want a girl or a boy?"

"Boy!"

"No, no," someone would interject. "You have to say 'girl' *last,* and then she'll get it right."

"Melanie, do you want a boy or a girl?"

"Boy-girl!"

"Listen, Melanie. Boy or *girl?* Boy or GIRL?"

"No!"

She finally got it "right" about six days before my due date, confessing under torture (they dangled a cookie over her head) that she wanted another sister.

A moment of triumph was planned for the octave after the little princess's birth. The girls would don their pink uniforms and march on parade. They toyed with the idea of each wearing a different word that would spell a message to the opinionated public: "It's Another Girl Yahoo Pffllt!" Melanie would wear the "!"

Greg assured me that all would be well in spite of these forebodings. We agreed not to tell the girls, but in the meantime we'd start preparing.

"Er . . . What are you gonna do if it's a boy?" I asked cautiously.

"Then we'll wear black!" retorted the General.

Right then and there I almost told them. Maybe they needed to know, in order to have time to adjust. I mean, God in His wisdom had ordained that I find out. He must have wanted me to be prepared. Should we do the same for the girls?

But Greg and I wanted them to have fun with the surprise. We stuck with the plan.

"You know, you've told everybody you *don't* want a boy. And that's not really true, is it? Now, what if it *is* a boy — how would you feel about declaring that?"

"It won't be," they said.

"But just what if?" I persisted. "Will you . . . like him?"

"Of course we would like him!"

I sighed in relief.

"But it isn't going to happen."

"Well, look. Just in case it does, you need to stop telling everybody you want a girl. Just say you want whomever God sends. God decides these things, and He has always known best. Isn't that the real message here? Girl or boy — God decides and we are happy?"

"Okay." They looked at each other knowingly as if to say, *we'll humor her.*

In the meantime I started preparing for the little guy.

I bought a boy's christening outfit on eBay and hid it away in my closet. There was no way I was going to put any son of mine into a satin gown, even if he wouldn't remember it.

Then I began making discreet inquiries among my friends. I approached one woman who had an only boy among four sisters. He seemed normal enough. Turns out her husband, too, had been the only boy. Normal again — unless you count the fact that he understood women's feelings.

I also approached a young priest of my acquaintance. "Let Greg raise him," was his advice. Greg — whose idea of a date movie is *The Godfather*? Sound counsel. The priest, a former Army captain, also offered to throw a ball with him. "Have the girls play ball with him, too," he said glancing over at the teens as they giggled and posed for pictures to put on Facebook for the millionth time. "It won't hurt them."

Yeah. It might even help. At that point they knew enough about sports to design T-shirts for sale in foreign countries. I used to see these things at open-air markets in Italy.

Amerikan Football
Yankes 10
Fliers 93

Okay: what to do in the event of a male invasion — *check*.

I also had a pretty good idea of what *not* to do. Take, for instance, the family at my daughters' co-op. They have a seven-year-old only boy. (Admittedly, he does resemble a cherub.) Unable to resist temptation, his sisters put him up on stage at every school event. They give him a microphone and accompany him on the piano while he sings cutesy songs. The audience gushes.

Bleah. What *not* to do — *check*.

Then Greg and I went on to the problem of names. It wasn't that we couldn't find one we liked; it was that we couldn't narrow it down. With the girls, we'd obviously had plenty of time to use up our supply of favorite names.

For the Boy, as far as Greg was concerned, nothing would do but the whole litany.

Unto Us a Son Is Born

Not wanting to make the girls suspicious, we went to a diner so we could discuss it in private.

"Peter," Greg said. "We should name him for the feast that falls near his birthday."

"But we don't have a special devotion to St. Peter," I objected. "Now here are the saints I like . . ."

"Saints you like!" my husband scoffed. "Hah! Just name the child according to your whims. Be like the rest of the world!"

"The rest of the world names their kids Traylor and Trellis. Catholics name their kid after saints they have a devotion to."

Still, something inside me said, *the guy's been outnumbered all this time. Let him name the baby.* "Since Peter is your middle name," I said. "We could name him after you if you like. If you really want that name, I'll give up one of mine."

He looked at my list.

St. Thomas More: patron of laymen
St. Edmund Campion: patron of Jebbies (Jesuits)
    and counter-reformers
St. Joseph: patron of Lloyds
And St. John Bosco: patron of boys

"You don't have to give anything up. We could name him Joseph Peter Thomas Campion John."

"Wait a minute," I said. "Three's the limit."

"Who says?"

"It's just that all those names will get lost."

"Nonsense." He kept on writing. A minute later his list had Joseph, Peter, Thomas, Campion, John, and Karl (after the last ruling Hapsburg — big favorite of ours).

"We can't give one child all those names! Why don't we just adopt a few more . . ."

9

"You know, I really like Paul." He scribbled some more.

When he was done, he had added Paul, Gregory, Vincent, Francis, Ferdinand, and Otto.

"Who the heck is Ferdinand?"

He didn't answer. He was fixated on his list. "John Bosco," he said thoughtfully. "You know, I've always loved Dominic Savio." He added Dominic.

"Look," I said. "Why don't we just pretend he's a member of the royal family? Or maybe there's some way we can sum them all up . . . we could just call the kid 'Martyr.' "

Greg reflected on this, and wrote down *Et Omnes Sanctos.* "Nah, doesn't have a ring to it. Tell you what," he said. "I'll compromise. Let's just stop at Karl."

"That still makes six! I'm wise to what you're doing. You're heaping them on so I'll agree to four. Well, it won't work!"

I don't know how we got home safely. We were both drunk on names.

Back in our kitchen, we dizzily staggered up to the calendar. St. Patrick's Day was near the proposed baptismal date. Great. How could I forget St. Patrick, in this half-Irish clan? Then there was St. Benedict, founder of western monasticism, lurking a couple of squares away.

"Benedict — we could name him for our Pope!" Greg said in a sloshy voice.

"Nah, we're already doing Joseph . . . Thash good enough. Hey, here'sh one. How about Ides?"

"St. Ides?" said Greg.

"The Ides of March. Julius ish a beautiful name."

"Or Ferial," he hiccoughed.

"Oh look — there'sh an Ember Day. Ember is such an original-sounding name. We could shtart a trend."

Unto Us a Son Is Born

The girls walked in. "I thought you were naming her *Serena!*"
Greg sobered up first. "*Maria . . .*" he teased. "I've always loved
that name."
"Come on, Dad, we know a *zillion* of them. We don't know *any*
Serenas."
"Okay," he said. "Maria Serena."
"No — Serena Maria!"
I went outside to rub snow in my face.
On February 23, two days late, I brought forth Joseph Peter
Charles. It was Greg's forty-fifth birthday. He phoned the girls
from my room. I heard screams. Some of them were crying. Others
were speechless.
Later that day they all trooped into the hospital, bearing gifts . . .
and wearing *blue*. They gazed down at the strange foreigner in the
little blue hat.
He was pretty, there was no doubt about it. His skin was
smooth, his head was round, he had fair peachy hair. But his nose
was masculine, and about the temples he looked like a boy.
They took turns holding him, cooing at him, claiming him. He
weighed all of eight and a half pounds. And yet I pictured him
someday towering over them, teasing them, protecting them.
He fit right in.

∞

Extra Vomitum, Nulla Parens

You're not really a parent until you have made contact with barf — or rather, until it has made contact with you. Until then you are merely a catechumen: a believer in the mysteries of parenthood, but not a full member of the club.

Unlike other rites of initiation, you don't invite people over to share in your joy. And you can't exactly plan the moment — the ceremony is traditionally performed without warning, in the middle of the night. The preferred method is full immersion, but it is also deemed sufficient to have it land on you.

It was many years ago when Greg and I were thus admitted to full communion of parenthood. We invited our second child, then three, into our bed.

"Honey, do you feel sick?"

She responded with a silent, violent nod of the head. In the next instant all our bedding became curb decor.

Greg and I looked at the mess. Our eyes met. It was as if we had shared a sacramental moment; God coming down and saying, "Congratulations, you two. You are now full members in the body of parenthood." (The heavenly host bursts into applause.)

But afterward we felt like Adam and Eve, the first parents to be thus driven from a warm bed. Sure, we had passed from ignorance to knowledge. We also had about a thousand years of cleanup.

Time passed. After a few years and a few more kids, we got complacent about barf. It no longer packed the same drama. Greg got used to sleeping on the floor beside the girls' beds, a large orange bucket the only thing between the sick child and his snoring head. I grew so accustomed to wading knee-deep in mire that, like the mothers of Genesis in the days of Noah, I was completely unprepared for the Deluge.

Let's see, it was our fifth child this time. She was lying on the couch. The couch was resting on the carpet. People were eating and drinking, marrying and giving in marriage. All was peace and quiet. Then, it was upon us. She bolted upright, "I feel yucky!"

"Do you want to throw up?"

"No!" she cried. (Kids are so literal. Of course she didn't *want* to. What kid does?)

I had to think quickly. The bathroom was upstairs. The nearest bucket was downstairs. The carpet was clean. So I rushed over, threw open my arms in the shape of a cross, and commanded, "Throw up on me!"

No sacrifice is too great to save carpeting and upholstery.

As I showered off later, I reflected that it was my own fault. Unlike most natural disasters or acts of God, I'd had fair warning. She *had* said a few words about feeling sick, just after losing her breakfast that morning. I should have started an ark right then. Or at least sent for the customary bucket-and-towel kit.

Why didn't I? Call it the effects of Original Sin. Weakness of the will, darkening of the intellect, never being prepared for a code-red disaster.

Extra Vomitum, Nulla Parens

I am sure there is a spiritual reason for it. Perhaps God means it for my betterment. I'm one of the women in the parable who put off running to Home Depot to get extra oil for her lamp. When the knock came at the door, the room was dark and somebody was throwing up on her.

It ought to teach preparedness at least. In the meantime, we will bear the dark and wet of night, hoping that somehow this, too, leads to salvation.

Is That Icon Frowning at Me?

Most of us, when we enter a church, can sense the Divine Presence. The red light flickers silently. There is a faint lingering scent of incense in the air. Our voices hush; we gingerly dip our fingertips into the holy water and quietly make our way to a vacant pew.

That's about where our toddler blurts out, "Are we going to church? I thought we were going to a diner!"

But that's okay. She prays like an angel — for about twenty-three seconds. She walks up to the front of our Byzantine parish church, kisses the icon, folds her wee dear hands, and mumbles, "Jesush, I *losh* you. Hep me be good."

After that there is nothing to do but wait until it's over. When you're three, this feels like forever and ever amen. "Is it over yet?" "No, Sweetie, Father hasn't even come out. Sit still and hush."

"I have to go to a bashroom." At home when she makes this announcement, it brings down the house. People come running from all directions. That's because at home she waits until the last minute to mention it.

At church it's just an excuse to go downstairs. I shake my head at her. Translation: "Try again in an hour." "I have to go to a bashroom!" She shimmies back and forth to convince me.

An older kid moves to get up and whispers, "I have to go anyway." I frown. Translation: "Sure, kid."

The priest emerges. That breaks up the monotony a little.

Now, we attend the full Ukrainian treatment, the typical duration of which is about three days (longer during Lent). But we're prepared. After all these kids, I ought to know how to keep them occupied during the Divine Liturgy. I've got a package of tissues for the baby to chew on, and a set of car keys to take away from him a second after he gets them and starts whacking the pew with them. For the three-year-old, a short stack of holy books. She's all geared up for the holy books because we'd been keeping them from her in the car so they'd be fresh and exciting. We hand them over, she grabs them greedily, flips through them in under a minute, and then starts pulling out her hair bows.

She then looks around at the congregation — people standing quietly, the occasional wink in her direction. Not much going on there. But who knows what will come? Once, the incense overpowered somebody and she got to see a little fainting action.

Nope. These are not the days of the midnight fast, and it appears everybody's eaten his Wheaties this morning. So my raggedy waif slithers under the pew to play with peoples' feet. That gets boring. Time to stand up on the pew. Better. Her sisters make faces as they repeatedly pull her down. Up. Down. Up. Down. Pinch. "Don't hurt me!" she shrieks.

Hark! Some old folks are caught sympathizing from behind. Time to ham it up. Pout, shy smile, grin, bounce up and down, wave wildly. Translation: "This is fun! If I climb over there, maybe that lady will give me some money."

We're now twenty minutes into the Divine Liturgy. Father is just beginning to consider that some time in the not-too-distant future he will prepare to read the Gospel.

Is That Icon Frowning at Me?

When I was new to the Eastern Rite, it appeared to me to be all *middle*; I couldn't decipher the Liturgy of the Word from the Liturgy of the Eucharist. It seemed to be nonstop chanting, punctuated with the all-occasion response: "Lord, have mercy."

> For good weather, an abundance of the fruits of the earth and for peaceful times: *Lord, have mercy.*

> For seafarers and travelers, the sick, the suffering, and for those held captive: *Lord, have mercy.*

> For an angel of peace, a faithful guardian of our souls and bodies: *Lord, have mercy.*

The signal that we're nearing the finish is: *Lord, have mercy. Lord, have mercy. Lord, have mercy. Give the blessing!*

It's been years now, and I have learned to understand the Eastern Liturgy and appreciate its rich beauty. The kids, too, have learned to treat it with great reverence, although at first they were prone to whisper and chatter. I helped break them of this habit by replying out loud, "YES? WHAT IS IT?"

Translation: "Want to cower under the pew? Keep talking."

I hate to confess that I stopped my husband from communicating the same way. I had to. He was talking to me from across the aisle.

In Eastern-rite churches the tradition is for the men to sit on one side in front of the icon of Jesus. The women sit on the other in front of the icon of the Blessed Mother — whose only child did *not* kick the pews. With six female children and an infant, this means that I get stuck with everybody.

The fact that only a handful of babushkas still do this makes it even more appealing to my favorite Irishman. Traditional *and* unpopular? Sold!

Yet the same Irishman also has the urgent need to communicate with me at all times. (The exception being when I say, "Let's talk.") He calls me when I'm having coffee with friends. He calls the neighbors when the phone at home is busy, and has them deliver messages to me. In church, when — by his own choice — he's sitting across the aisle from, he goes, "Pssst!"

I know what he wants. The priest is intoning the name of the Blessed Trinity, and Greg wants to remind me to show the girls to bow reverently and make the Sign of the Cross with three fingers together. I pretend to be immersed in prayer. Translation: "You sit all the way over there and leave me alone with seven kids, and *now* you want to talk?"

"Susie," he mumbles. I turn to him and say in a normal conversational tone, "WHAT?" He rolls his eyes and gestures at the kids, pantomimes the Sign of the Cross, and bows. I stare back blankly.

He motions for me to send a couple of them over there. The seven- and twelve-year-old look at me pleadingly, their shiny church shoes cemented to the floor. Translation: "Walk across the aisle in front of everybody? Ugh!" He motions again and they obey. The migration phase has begun.

The toddler notices and tries to follow. She's been dying for a chance to play musical pews. Under our former system, when our family was all in one pew, Greg would sit at one end and I at the other, thus forming a barrier to No Man's Land. Now, under the traditional, liturgically correct, near-occasion-of-sin system, the children are free to run back and forth between the pews. Greg doesn't mind. It gives him a chance to relay messages to me.

Pew-hopping reaches its height during Lenten prostrations. In that season we sing a series of dirges about the Cross and then bow low and kiss the floor. To the three-year-old it's the most wonderful time of the year. It means going out into the aisle with Dad, throwing herself on the floor three times, ruffled backside in the air, exuding sweetness and piety. Old folks produce money.

At times I've tried to avoid all of this by standing in the back. You can't sit there — the back pews are taken by old people who camp out the night before to get them. But why they want them, I'll never know. Do *they* suddenly climb up on the pew and start babbling and jumping up and down? "Stop it, Mildred! You're distracting people!"

But I don't care. I'll take my penance and stand. I leave my pew carrying a squalling child who is wiggling out of my grip like an overflowing bag of groceries with a hole in it. I'm bending over, grabbing him with my arms, legs, and chin, and he's still spilling out. The old people grin as we go by — isn't he cute?

The three-year-old sees, hustles out of Daddy's pew, and patters down the aisle to catch up. Do I send her back? No, I don't want to risk the Boomerang Effect. So now I have two of them.

The baby amuses himself for a few minutes by dumping out the collection baskets. Then he heads for the steps leading up to the choir.

I swoop him up and plant him back where he started. Translation: "Forget it, kid. You're staying put." He toddles back again. Translation: "Make me." Swoop: "I said forget it." Back again: "Oh yeah, just try to keep up with me." Swoop. I lock my arms around him. "Waaah!"

Great. How do you lock up a scream?

Lord, have mercy . . .

I put him down. He forgets the stairs and starts pulling the freestanding flags down on himself.

Lord, have mercy . . .

He spies holy cards in a back pew, wobbles over, grabs a handful, and starts chewing.

21

Bless Me, Father, for I Have Kids

Lord, have mercy . . .

One of the old back-pew campers pats him on the head. He feels affirmed. Now he wants to see the rest of the church. Off he goes, straight up the center aisle.

Lord, have mercy. Lord, have mercy. Lord, have mercy. Give the blessing already!

Never Drive Faster Than
Your Guardian Angel Can Fly

My husband insists on doing all the driving. It's part old-fashioned chivalry and part fear that someone will see him in the passenger seat and think he got a DUI.

Many years ago, his siblings dubbed him Mototrend — an insult he's proud of to this day.

He lives the dream. We first started dating in Liechtenstein — national motto: Our highway system was designed by cows. Now, these were very smart German-engineered cows. When these cows got together and looked over the plans, somebody mooed that rambling straight down such steep, tall hills could cause their backsides to go hurtling over their heads. Hence, it was concluded that they would meander first to the right, then to the left, then right, then left, and so on. By the time they reached the bottom of the hill, they had added ten extra miles but were alive and in tip-top condition for the slaughterhouse. Their descendants still travel the same roads today, leaving mounds of stinky hay behind them.

Greg got himself an international driver's license just so he could follow in their hoofsteps at about ninety miles per hour.

Bless Me, Father, for I Have Kids

Roaring down the cowpaths in his best pal's tiny tin Peugeot, the bald tires struggling to find grip, was how he first got me to throw my arms around him. That we've lived to tell about it is a tribute to his driving skills and my prayers to the guardian angels.

Greg tells me there was nothing to be afraid of — he was in complete control. And that is true to this day. While Greg is driving, he not only pilots the vehicle but insists on personally adjusting all buttons designed for the comfort of the passengers.

"Who closed the vent?!" he asks.

"I did," I own up. "The air was drying my eyeballs out."

"Well, kindly keep your hands to yourself. *I* am driving. *I am the car.*"

"I was cold, too."

"Kids, hand that blanket up from the trunk." He throws it on my lap. "Here, wear my hat." He pulls it down over my eyes.

"I'm not *that* cold. It's sixty-five degrees out. I just don't like the draft."

"Okay, okay," he says, sighing. (Translation: She's *so* impossible.) "Allow me . . ."

Through a series of deft movements he manipulates the heating system. Result — my vent is closed.

The next thing we do, if going on a trip of any length, is to say the Rosary. The car is a particularly efficient place to say Rosaries. For one thing, everybody is tied down — literally.

Kids can't scoot across the floor on their knees, pilgrimage-style, to get away from someone who is poking them. You are staring at the backs of people's heads, not at their other ends while their faces are buried in the sofa. Decades can't be killed off by bathroom visits. Unlike our in-house Rosaries, wherein work-exhausted Dad falls asleep during the Sign of the Cross, in the car he is alert and ready. Instead, the baby is the one who falls asleep.

"Now, did you all remember to wear your parachutes?"

Bless Me, Father, for I Have Kids

You'll agree that this is preferable to being hit over the head with blunt objects.

But it's not perfect either.

Praying is tough when there's static interference. This happens when a small child in the back row is leading a decade, and in the middle of a Hail Mary, turns her head.

"Hail Mary . . . the . . . blessed . . . fruit . . . Jesus."

Emergency broadcast system kicks in from all corners of the car. "Speak up!"

Dad won't stand for it. "Leave her alone. She's doing fine."

"But she's fading in and out, and it's driving everybody crazy."

"I said leave her alone, Mommy. Now girls, have patience with your little sister. Do you want our Lord to have patience with you?"

The sermon begins. Expect delays.

We pray most fervently on Sunday mornings, when a) we are commanded to honor the Lord, b) we are late for Mass, and c) we fear for our lives.

Although normally I am not allowed to touch anything, but instead must sit still on my wifely pedestal in the passenger seat, wearing a blanket and a hat, it's different when we're running late. Greg expects me to co-pilot. This is a very important job when you are attempting to fly a full-size van. Mototrend doesn't bother taxiing. We achieve liftoff as soon as we peel away from the curb. My first job: adjust the mirrors.

"You know, *you* drove the van last," I remind him. "How can the mirror be wrong?"

"It jiggles when you slam the door."

Meanwhile we're driving through our quiet development faster than the kids can say Hail Marys from the back seat. The window is rolled down, I'm still fixing the mirrors. Moto wants them just right.

"Up a bit. No, no. Now down. That's . . . pretty good. Now just out a bit farther . . ." My primped and sprayed church hairdo is now in a series of knots that Alexander the Great couldn't untie with a sword. *Will the mortician be able to get this undone?* I wonder. I don't want the mourners to gasp, "What was she thinking with that hair?"

By the time we reach the highway ramp, we're cruising at 5,000 feet and Greg starts looking for cops.

"Any bears in the air?"

"If you're using CB code to keep the kids from knowing you're on the wrong side of the law, it's too late." Cue the kids.

"Dad! We almost lost Gracie that time!"

"She's skinny. She's getting sucked right out the seat belt!"

"Close the window!" I holler over the noise of the engines. "It destabilizes the air pressure in the cabin."

"Don't any of you children touch that window," he calls back. We have the perfect cross-draft of air." He turns to me. "Can you do something about them?"

"Quiet. You're interrupting my meditation on the four last things."

"You just look for bears."

He has now promoted me to air-traffic controller. In all these years, I have yet to spot one police helicopter. I think the state puts the blue signs up purely as a deterrent. Oh well, it's the thought that counts. I humor him and squint upward. "You passed one a minute ago, but he was helping one of the Blue Angels with wing trouble."

"Where?" He suddenly eases up on the gas. "I don't see anything. Oh, very funny. Come on now, I'm serious. Do you want to get to Mass before the Gospel? What if I get a ticket? You want me to pay two hundred dollars?"

Copilot: stand by and nag. "If that's what it takes, I'm all for it. We go through this all the time. How hard could it be to leave on time for once?"

"Quiet, my radar detects an enemy approach." It's a small yellow vehicle with black tinted windows. In a matter of nanoseconds, it closes in, rides our rear, flashes its lights, honks, and as soon as there's an opening, passes on the right. Just in case we missed the point, a large hairy arm emerges from the window and gives the one-finger salute.

The temperature suddenly goes up in the cabin as Greg reacts. "This genius knows sign language! Can you believe these people?" He rolls down the window. "HEY, GENIUS — GO BACK TO NEW YORK!"

Then silence. Nothing except the nervous babble — "pray for us sinners, now and at the hour . . ." — from the back seat.

His countenance softens. He slows the van to sixty-five. He is no longer Mototrend. He is resigned to walk into Sunday Mass late but chastised, humble, and gratefully alive.

"There go I but for the grace of God . . ."

∞

Mrs. Murphy's Law

Any parents with a big family have asked themselves, "Is it worth it?"

To me, "it" can mean only one thing: taking all the kids out in public at one time.

Back when I was a young mother with only two adjectives to describe my children — *small* and *numerous* — I used to attempt to go out in public with all of them, but little by little, I had to give it up. Even if it meant doing without certain luxuries, such as food. (Hey, we'd still go out on Sundays — the day God makes you go to church with all the kids to keep you humble.)

I stayed home for two reasons:

1. People would go into shock at the mere sight of us, like this woman at the dry cleaner. Pierced tongue, eyebrow stud, tattoos down to her wrists, and she says, "Six girls! Lady, what were you thinking?!"

Lady, what was *I* thinking?

2. Murphy's Law (Mrs. Murphy, that is — an Irish Catholic with ten kids): *Anything that can go wrong will go wrong in front of other people.* When disaster strikes at home, you have your very

own bathtub and Lysol nearby. In public all you have is a restroom sink, and hopefully a lock on the door.

The last time Greg and I took the kids to Friendly's was literally that: the last time. It was crowded, as usual. So far, so good — we fit right in. Then our two-year-old at the time — who requests that her birth number remain anonymous — created her very own pond in the highchair.

Rule number one when you are in that situation: Do not alert the staff. Once, at a fine restaurant when somebody's kid threw up, Greg and I witnessed how hospitality professionals handle delicate situations like this. They point at it and scream, "EEEW!"

Do not, I repeat, alert the staff. Do this instead:

• *Step one:* Simply drag the highchair into the bathroom as if it's nothing. Your attitude should say, "Don't all customers take highchairs into bathrooms with them?" Dump contents of high chair into toilet. Scrub with peroxide, ammonia, or alcohol, which should be located in handy dispensers on the wall. If unavailable, use soap, water, and paper towels. In the event there's no soap, pour gasoline on highchair and ignite.

• *Step two:* At the same time as step one, have an older child swiftly and quietly remove wet tot to the car. Child should wait until inside the car to yell, "Why the heck didn't you go at home?!"

• *Step three:* Pay bill and exit with remaining dry children.

• *Step four:* Stay home for at least two more years or until all potty accidents are behind you. Then stay home after that. If you're expecting more children, you may wish to become self-supporting. Grow crops, raise cattle, learn to build rabbit traps.

Mrs. Murphy's Law

Unless, of course, you get yourself a teenager.

Most of us foolishly had small children before having teenagers. This is all wrong. I don't advise it. Veteran parents agree, although I'm still not sure if it's easier than raising cattle.

These medium-size people may be expensive, but consider: isn't an I-pod, a PC, or ridiculously high car insurance worth it? For not only do teens have control over most of their bodily functions; they are also fully equipped to babysit small people. This enables full-size people to go out to a fine restaurant for a relaxing time away, to enjoy watching other people's two-year-olds throw up next to them. "EEEW!"

But even if you are careless, as most of us were, and you accidentally have children without benefit of teenagers, take heart. These children will eventually grow into teenagers. On that day, you can stop scratching tally marks on the walls of your kitchen. You are sprung. Go out to the grocery store by yourself. Stand boldly alone in the candy aisle. Find out who abducted Angelina's clone aboard Nostradamus's future-ship. Breathe the fresh scent of asphalt again!

My day is here. And I must say it was worth getting a lot older, because now I feel young again. I've even started dressing younger. I no longer need a set of jean jumpers serviceable for climbing under clothing racks. Back to the thrift store whence they came — now it's straighter, knee-length jean skirts.

What? You were expecting leopard skin? Hey, I'm still people's mother, and therefore must look respectable. Although, for fun one day I did pull on a pair of black leather boots, over dark stockings. I then sported this get-up at a spot known for attracting cute, young males. One of them ran up to me in the pet-food aisle and said, "Hey, *Senora*, my dad thinks you're beautiful!"

Okay, so he was six. I must admit, it made my day. My day! I rather liked the sound of that.

Bless Me, Father, for I Have Kids

My teens didn't. They walked ten feet behind me saying, "Where'd Mom go?" The other would shrug, "I don't know — let's ask that floozy up ahead if she's seen her."

Nowadays I am so used to my liberty that from time to time I forget how it was in the dark days before teenagers. One Christmas, I planned an outing to see *The Nutcracker* with my then-six children, ages two and up. No problem, I thought. We're going with a bunch of homeschoolers; people will think we're a school. Tongue-pierced dry cleaners will not gawk in horror. Not only that: there were three teens to help me manage the then-two-year-old (also to remain numberless; not Puddlepants mentioned earlier).

Naturally the teens sat in different places in the theater and left the baby to me. For the next hour and a half she did more dancing than anybody on stage. All she needed was a caller:

*Climb down off your mama's lap/Poke the kid in front of you
Mama swing yer toddler up/Bounce her on your knee
Sashay left, sashay right —
Kick your mama in the shins/Roll away now to the floor!
Go see sister. Promenade —
Dive on through. U-turn back. Climb back up. Stand on lap
Kick your mama/Squirm some more —
Now you jump down to the floor!
Step on her left foot/Now on her right . . .*

Now repeat . . .

Sixteen seats down and one row ahead, I spied hope. My maternal radar picked up a signal from a roll of Smarties glowing in my ten-year-old's pocket. How to get at these sedatives? Four seats down sat one of the teens. "Pssst!" I tried to get her attention. Suddenly she seemed keenly interested in a bunch of dancing sugarplums. I whispered to her to get the Smarties. This child, who does not deserve to remain anonymous,* refused on the grounds that she didn't want to make a scene. I threatened to make one for her. She got the Smarties.

The two-year-old then settled into my lap, and in a few moments, for the first time that day, a feeling of warmth and comfort flooded over me. Then, just as quickly, it cooled off.

Turned out the child assigned to get the kid ready (Number One — ha) had neglected to change her diaper, and it had just exceeded capacity. On stage was the finale, the moment we'd all been waiting for, wherein a gigantic gingerbread woman (actually a big ugly guy in drag) rolls onto the stage and appears to give birth to eight little gingerbread children (no teens — good luck). I spent it in the bathroom, holding a pair of wee stockings in front of the hand dryer and pondering my fragile sanity.

You see, the outing was far from over. I had promised to take the whole gang plus an additional family to McDonald's Playland.

Before leaving the restroom, I took one last look in the mirror. My reflection looked back and smiled wryly as if to say: "Lady, what were you thinking?"

*She is Number Two.

∞

Murder in the Kitchen: A *Musical*

Training the kids to take chore duty seriously is one of parent-hood's biggest challenges. It helps if the parent is organized. A friend of mine uses a large chart with each child's name beside a chore, corresponding to each day of the week. It is all very professional.

My method is strictly managerial. I point to a mess and assign the nearest child caught doing nothing (chewing, reading, walking through the room with an armload of laundry) to clean it up. The exception being dishes. When the three eldest were still the size of dwarves, it was necessary to rotate dishes in order to be fair.

The problem was no one could ever agree on whose turn it was. Scrubby was the leader and every night would dictate that it was not her turn. Soapy, the youngest, would insist that she had done them the night before last, and therefore it was Suds's turn. Suds was "frankly sick of getting stuck in the middle" and was "not going to be the nice guy!"

They played the scene so many times I thought they were going to take it on tour.

Any minute I expected a Greek chorus to enter and start chanting:

Bless Me, Father, for I Have Kids

'Twas at night after supper
and all through the kitchen
the kids made excuses
not to pitch in.

There was plenty of stage combat to go with it. Then Sweepie, the littlest of the working dwarves, but too small for dishes, would rush onto the stage and start shrieking.

Chorus:
Sweepie has no clue about what started this infraction
She's been cooped up in the house all day and needs
*   to see some action.*

The drama wouldn't end until I walked in as the *Deus ex machina* (only without hanging from the rafters) and delivered the final line: "There will be no arguing to the death. Bloodshed has been outlawed in this theater — executions, which are at the discretion of the director, excepted."

Then I'd hand out roles. Soapy to clear and put away food. Scrubby on dishes, Miss Suds on pots. Sweepie would reprise her number — sweep and the garbage, two bits. Baby worked as an extra, running around in the background for effect.

This performance was flawed. It depended too much on my directing. On nights when I couldn't be there, my husband substituted his magic show: leave the stage and shut off the lights, and the dirt disappears before your very eyes.

What we needed was a plan to bring the kids to independence.

I could just imagine them years hence, after my death, trying to contact me on the Other Side, like the Three Weird Sisters:

Tell us O mother of toil,
whose turn it is to scrub the soil?

But one night the girls surprised me. They had formed a committee to overthrow me as director of *Murder in the Kitchen*.

"Mom, rotating jobs is just not working. From now on, we each want to play the same part every night. That way we'll always know what to do. Everyone can just pick the part she hates least, learn it, and there will be no confusion. Besides, Suds says she'll pick up dishes and pots now that we have a dishwasher."

My first thought was to get Suds her own dressing room with a star on it. My next was to say, "What's my job?"

"You? Go take a walk with Dad. You'd just be in the way."

I couldn't believe it. After years of faithful service, they fired me, without so much as a letter of recommendation. They were so confident, so cold, so professional about it. It was wonderful!

But it became clear after a few performances that they weren't ready to go undirected yet. They called on me for consulting — a lot.

Suds: "Mom, tell the girls to do their jobs! Dinner's been over for an hour, and the food is petrifying."

Soapy: "That's because *she* won't empty the dishwasher and get me some clean Tupperware."

Scrubby: "Well *she's* been dancing around in the living room while I've been clearing the table."

I'd have to go in and find out who missed what cue and was throwing everybody else off. Turns out it was a case of role-swapping. The committee had recently given Sweepie's role to Wee Debris — The Artist Formerly Known as Baby. Sweepie had been assigned a more demanding role, but she preferred to wait offstage in the bathroom for a half-hour and hope someone else would improv her routine.

One night Scrubby called an emergency meeting. The Abba CD blaring in the living room had given her an idea. Why not turn *Murder in the Kitchen* into a musical? Just think — the whole kitchen could be cleaned up in the time it takes to hear one song by the Swedish Chipmunks. The committee agreed.

She cued up the CD and yelled, "Go!"

Presenting: The Kitchen Five!

You can dance, you can jive, having the time of your life . . .

The girls run back and forth between rooms.

Night is young and the music's high . . .

Percussion: *clank, chip, crack!*

And when you get the chance . . . You are the dancing queen!

Cue the extras. The two toddlers want to get in on the act.

Leave them burning and then you're gone . . .

"Ooff!" Bodies collide into each other. Somebody shouts, "Who did I step on?"

Looking out for another, anyone will do . . .

"Wah!"

Dancing queen, feel the beat from the tambourine, oh yeah . . .

"Faster! The song's almost over!"

See that girl, watch that scene, diggin' the dancing queen . . .

Fade out.

The girls stop in their tracks. An imaginary curtain does down. There is silence. You could hear a soap bubble pop.

"We were so close," says Miss Suds, her shoulders sagging.

"Yeah," says Soapy, slumping into a chair.

"This was a dumb idea," adds Scrubby, staring at the floor as if expecting to see glass shards.

The rest of us burst into applause. "Bravo! Just look at this set. Gleaming countertops, glistening wet table, a salad bowl dripping in the dish rack. Troupe, don't throw in the towel. Encore! Encore!"

Murder in the Kitchen

The Kitchen Five look around the stage. All that remains to mar the scene is a scalded sauce pot, a garbage can without a liner, and a pile of crumbs lying beside a plastic dustpan — in which the smallest extra is foraging for Cheerios. All in all a good show — the result of just under four minutes' work.

Enter the Chorus to deliver the moral of the story: *If you must have Martha's dishpan hands, at least have a merry mind.*

∞

Carefree and Barely Three!

You tall-legged people think my life is easy. "Oh, that carefree age!" you say.

What's "carefree" about it? Potty-training was grueling. No wonder some of my friends are still holding out. Once I got past that, I thought the worst was over, but no, there's always some-thing *else* to learn — like not to stand up on my chair during sup-per. After that it'll be something else. It never ends.

Don't get me wrong. These past three years have been good to me. Very, very good. Tall-legged people smile at me a lot. One time I smiled back and this lady said, "She has a dimple!" I don't get it. What's a dimple?

Sometimes people give me presents. The lady at the bank gives me lollipops. One time an old lady at church gave me a dollar. All I had to do was say, "Thank you." Sometimes people wink at me for no reason. I can wink too. Wanna see? If I squint hard I can close one eye just for a second. People love it when I do that. They laugh, and then I get a fit of the giggles.

I hope this proves once and for all that I don't cry *all of the time*. My sisters say I do, but I don't! But hearing that *really* makes me want to cry. They say the same thing about Joey. I have to agree with them there. He cries *way, way* more than I do. You can be playing with him, and he'll be laughing; then suddenly he'll cry for no reason.

I *always* have a reason to cry: I had to wear the fountainhead hairdo to church. I got yelled at for painting the bed with nail polish. I'm not allowed to eat toothpaste . . .

You people have a lot of rules. I could tell you what's wrong with them, but I do not yet have full command of the English language. Soon, very soon.

And of course, when Joey cries, you pick him up and give him a drink. You kiss him or play with him or feed him. When I cry a lot, you put me to bed. That *really, really* makes me want to cry. You don't listen. I cry and scream, "No! I don' WANNA take a nap!" Then you say, "Oh, she really *is* tired."

Hello? I have plenty of energy. I'd stop crying if somebody would just *play with me.* My sisters play with me a little bit, then suddenly they're done. Just like that. So of course I cry. I've only just begun to play! Come on, let's roll on the floor! Let's jump off the couch! Let's crawl down the stairs on our stomachs!

Mommy and Daddy hardly ever play with me. They say they have work to do. I keep offering — "I wan' help!" But they never accept my assistance. They say, "Go play. That would be helping." *How?* How would that be helping? You don't make sense. Besides, nobody will play with me, remember?

I always hear them say that they are trying to make ends meet. What's so hard about that? I do it all the time! Do you need tape or glue? I've almost got the hang of the stapler. Let me help!

You have no idea how boring my life can get. I'm not allowed to have any hobbies. One time I colored the wall, and Mommy flipped out. She won't let me jump on the bed; instead she gives me books I can't read. The pictures are nice, but what I'd really like is to make towers out of them and jump off.

Carefree and Barely Three!

Why can't I have attention like the baby gets? All he has to do is look at Mommy and she picks him up and plays with him. She scoops him up and kisses him on the neck in the tickle spot. And it's not just Mommy. Daddy, the girls — they all do it.

Okay, I guess I do it, too. He *is* fun to play with. He runs around after me. He loves all my games. He's my groupie. I like having him around — except for when he pulls my hair, which makes me cry. (You'll agree that's a good reason to cry.) But I forgive him because you say he doesn't mean to hurt me. He doesn't know better. He's a baby, not a big girl like me. I don't paddle my hands in the toilet, for one thing. (The girls say I tried when I was little, but I don't believe it.) I don't spit cereal back at Mommy, drink bath water, or wave a huge stick at the cat and think it's funny. Well, when Joey does that it *is* pretty funny. But I shake my finger at him: "No, no!" That's my job.

That's what I like most about Joey — when I'm with him, I get to be the big girl. I can feed him if he holds still. I can climb on a chair to reach his bottle and not get yelled at. Best of all, I can rescue him. Like the time he got tangled up in the phone cords, I yelled, "Your baby's crying!" Mommy came running. Later she thanked me for it — said I was a big girl. Am I not wonderful at making announcements?

True, Mommy didn't thank me that time I stood next to the crib and hollered, "Joey can wake up now!" But I was so bored! No one would play with me. Anyway, forget about that incident. Try to remember the good moments, like that time I yelled, "Joey's in the toilet!"

At home I like to yell, but not when I go places. I'm quiet out in the big world. There are too many tall legs and loud voices. The rooms feel strange. I don't know what I'm allowed to do. I don't know what might suddenly happen. I need to stay close to people I know.

Bless Me, Father, for I Have Kids

Especially since I'm afraid to cry in front of strangers. That's new with me. Funny it never bothered me before. I was like Joey; if I fell down or someone bumped into me, I'd just let it all hang out. I couldn't help it. I'd be running, and my feet would get tangled. Sometimes I wasn't looking and I'd hit my head on a table. Don't you hate that?

But I forgot. You never do that. You tall-legged people *never* get hurt. Why is that? I get hurt like *every day*.

You pay lots of attention when I get hurt — all of you. Mommy sits down and rocks me, and the girls run and get toys. Daddy picks me up, and I get to ride around way up high. He points to a hole I made in the floor where I fell. I can never see it, but I look hard and forget about the hurt and stop crying. A couple of times I tried to make the attention last. Just kept crying and crying. But Mommy knew I was faking. How?

Sometimes I wish I could be like you tall-legged people, and never cry or get hurt. But then Mommy and Daddy wouldn't pick me up anymore, would they? They never pick up the big girls. They're too big. Would people still wink at me? Tall-legged people don't wink at each other.

Would I still get to sleep with Joey? In the morning Joey and I wake up and stare at each other, and he starts laughing for no reason. He bounces up and down in his crib. So I bounce up and down on my bed. It's so fun!

Once Mommy and Daddy and the girls heard us and came in. I pointed and screamed, "Look at Joey! He's so funny!" Then they swooped down and kissed me on my neck right in the tickle spot, and I giggled and giggled. Then somebody said it, "How lucky to be that carefree age!"

Hey . . . I think I get it now!

∞

The Perfect Family
A Fairy Tale

O nce there was a normal American family: a mommy, a daddy, and a baby daughter. Everywhere they went, people stopped them and said, "My, what a lovely baby!"

Mommy and Daddy were happy.

Then the normal American family had another baby daughter. The two babies used to ride together in a double stroller. Everywhere the family went, people stopped them and exclaimed, "Two girls. Oh, how nice. Are you going to try for a boy?"

Mommy and Daddy just shrugged and smiled at their two little girls. They were happy.

Not much time went by, and the family was blessed with another baby girl. Everywhere they went, people would stop them and say, "Oh my! Three girls. Are you going to stop now? Or are you going to hold out for a boy?"

Mommy and Daddy were beginning to get annoyed. They didn't like people telling them there was something wrong with their children. But they were sweet and kind at all times (hey, this is a fairy tale, kid). They never once considered turning anyone into a frog.

Instead, they just smiled. (Mommy was gritting her teeth, though.) Daddy winked at her. The wink meant: No biting people. As I said, they were happy.

Some time passed, and the family was blessed with another baby girl, then another, then another still. Six girls in all! Nobody thought of them as a normal American family anymore. Wherever they went, people stopped them and said, "Oh my! Six daughters. Yipes! Six weddings! Six bathrooms! You must be rich."

"No," said Mommy and Daddy firmly. "But we're happy."

In fact, Mommy was not happy. She was tired of strangers bugging her and Daddy about their children. One night Mommy and Daddy sat at the table after all the children were asleep. Mommy slammed the yellow pages down on the table. "Let's see," she said, flipping the pages. "Monsters, Ogres, Spells . . . ah — Voodoo Doctors!"

"Mommy, what are you thinking?!" said Daddy, horrified.

"I was just seeing if I could stop people from criticizing us for having lots of children — the *wrong kind* of children!"

"Just tell them we thank God and we're happy . . ." said Daddy. "And if that doesn't work, you could turn yourself into a hag and hawk poisoned apples."

"Would you be serious? I have to figure something out fast," said Mommy. "Because there will soon be another one!" (Mommy's level of hysterione, the pregnancy hormone, had just reached "Tsunami.")

"There, there," said Daddy, removing the phone book from her teeth. "God will help us."

It just so happened that a fairy was watching. Her name was Ditzy. Ditzy was a kindhearted fairy who loved to help people. But she wasn't the brightest wand in the aurora. You see, she didn't really listen to the people she was trying to help. Instead she rushed in with a quick fix that usually didn't work out.

Once, when she was filling in for the tooth fairy, she heard a little boy say that he hoped he'd get a hundred dimes for his tooth. So later that night, when she appeared in his bedroom and found the tooth under his pillow, she stuck a hundred dimes in his mouth where the tooth used to be. When the boy woke, he begged Ditzy to reverse the spell, but it was too late: Ditzy had an All Spells Are Final policy. The boy left home to make his fortune in a circus sideshow and lived happily never after.

After that, the Elder Fairies gave her the unflattering name of Ditzy, suspended her, and put her on the list of registered hex offenders. Ditzy was terribly ashamed of it. She wanted more than anything to get back into full-time fairy work.

And so the night she heard Mommy and Daddy talking, she hit on a plan. "Monsters, ogres, voodoo doctors — pooh!" she said. "Why bother with those dark forces? What Mommy and Daddy need is a fairy. Whoever this God person is, He doesn't seem to know what He's doing. Six girls!" (Ditzy did not share Mommy and Daddy's idea of a normal American family.) But she needed time to think of a plan, and with her slow head it could take a while.

A few months later, the family had their baby — a boy this time. All the girls were thrilled. Mommy and Daddy were thrilled. A little brother — what a blessing! Now, wherever the family went, people stopped them and said, "You finally made it! You got your boy!" Then they would look at the girls and shudder, "Seven kids — what a nightmare!"

Mommy started to bare her fangs, but Daddy stopped her and said, "Which ones should we send back?"

Ditzy was listening. Now she finally knew exactly what she'd do! She would help make the family better than normal — she would make it *perfect*! She was so excited she could hardly wait for the family to go to sleep, so she could work her magic.

Mommy and Daddy didn't sleep well that night. They tossed and turned. There was something wrong. The house was too still and quiet. There was no sound of children pounding up the stairs after their movie ended past midnight. No slamming of the basement door by teens washing clothes they needed for the next day. No boomerang children jumping out of bed because they forgot to brush their teeth.

When day came, Mommy and Daddy went to check on the children.

First they checked the nursery. There was their little baby boy sleeping soundly in his crib. Next to him in her toddler bed was their little girl.

They called upstairs to the other five children. But there was no answer. "They must be sleeping," said Daddy. And he called louder.

"Good morning, Perfect Family!" said a strange voice. Mommy and Daddy looked up. There at the top of the stairs was Ditzy, all dressed up and looking very pleased with herself. "Like the pink and blue tutu?" she grinned. "I conjured it just for the occasion."

"Who are you?" gasped Mommy and Daddy.

"Let's just call me the good fairy," said Ditzy. "You needn't bother to look upstairs. They aren't there anymore."

"Our children?!"

"Gone! No need to thank me. But if you insist . . ."

"What are you talking about?" they exclaimed.

As usual, Ditzy wasn't listening. "I got rid of their bunk beds too, the ones you hurt your back lugging up the stairs, Daddy. While I was at it, I sent the hundred and one stuffed Dalmatians — the ones you always complain about, Mommy — right out the window. *Poof!*

"There will be no more clothes littering the floor, and no papers, keychains, stickers, hair bows, chopsticks, and Barbie parts jammed into dresser drawers. Yuck. Oh, Mommy — remember that time you lined the three teens up at the orthodontist and asked, 'Which one needs braces the most?' Those days are over! How about the time you wanted to sign one of them up for Irish Dancing but didn't because then you'd have to send the others and you couldn't afford more than one? Now you can! Your little girl will look so cute in the wee orange dress. And him! Your young prince can have baseball, soccer, and tae kwon do all at the same time. And he won't have to grow up with, you know, *all* those sisters.

"Best of all," continued Ditzy, "now you can hold your head up proudly when people compliment you on your beautiful children. Admit it, Mommy: you get mad at Daddy for telling people you have seven children, because you're tired of sitting through their fainting spells."

Mommy hung her head, ashamed. It was true. If Ditzy knew that, even with her silly head, everyone else probably did, too.

Ditzy moved closer, put her arm around Mommy, and said sympathetically, "Those days are no more!" She touched Mommy gently on the head with her wand. "You are one of *them* now. You fit in."

But at the touch of her wand, Mommy recoiled. "I don't *want* to fit in. I was happy with the way it was. Even with the clutter!"

"Oh, come now," replied Ditzy a little impatiently. "Haven't you've secretly longed to put your desk in the nursery, so you can work in peace and quiet, instead of in your bedroom, where you always whack your leg against the furniture? Well, it's yours. Besides, every child should have his own room. It's the American dream. And Daddy, your car worries are over. You can sell the Clampett-mobile to a less fortunate family, or donate it to a Pentecostal church. Get yourselves something sporty and start having fun."

"You don't understand," said Daddy, trying to be patient, for he could see that the fairy was ditzy. "We were having fun. Lots of fun. Just watching the kids grow up was fun for us."

"You can still have fun," said Ditzy. "Think quality, not quantity. You've got — ahem, thanks to me — what all parents dream of: a boy and a girl. You've got the perfect family!"

"Are you even listening?" said Daddy, less patient now. "We have been trying to tell you that we already *had* the perfect family."

"Yes, and we want it back!" said Mommy fiercely.

"Sorry — no can do! Once done is done forever. Ever hear of Jo-Jo the Dime-Faced Boy? Because of me he's rich and famous! I call that a satisfied customer. Only," she continued, her face darkening, "*they* don't think so. In Fairyland, they called it a Big Mistake. They took away my status, my job, and even my name. They," she started whimpering, "they called me . . ."

"What?" said Mommy and Daddy.

"Never you mind," said the fairy, drawing herself up. "If I told you, it would break the spell. And, Mommy, I know you wouldn't like that. After all, you said you had the wrong kind of children. Don't try to deny it. I heard it with my own ears."

"I was just saying what other people think. Don't you listen? Or are you just lame-brained? That's not what *I* think. I love the children the way they are."

"Sure," said Ditzy sarcastically. "Just the way God made them, yadda yadda yadda. Huh — the *amateur!*"

"You know what you are?" said Daddy, finally losing his patience. "You are ditzy!"

Ditzy opened her mouth, but it was too late. Daddy had guessed her name. *Poof!* In that very instant, she disappeared, leaving behind only a puff of pink and blue smoke.

In her place at the top of the stairs appeared five grumpy girls in their pajamas, rubbing their eyes. "What'ya wake me up for?" said one. "Got anything to eat?" said another. The baby heard and started crying. The two-year-old came out of her room and called, "Whewe is evewybody?"

"We're all here!" said Mommy and Daddy. And they were happy.

The End

∞

A Little Lower Than the Angels . . .
Okay, a Lot Lower

∞

Handouts and Hand-Me-Downs

Greg and I have never had to have that little talk. You know, when the kids come of age, and sidle up to you and ask, "Mommy, Daddy, where does clutter come from?"

Ours already know. It's like being brought up on a farm. Cows and chickens come from other cows and chickens. Clutter, too, reproduces each after its own kind. There is nothing mysterious about it, and it's not evolution. People keep giving the stuff to us. Something goes off in their brains when they see a big family.

"Hon, quick! Get that huge metal table with the paint chipping off. The Lloyds left their van unlocked!"

One dear old friend had been hoarding holy cards like a pious dragon. He finally sent a spare vat-ful to us because "you can't throw these things out, you know." We know. We now own a complete set of the Communion of the Saints.

Most common are clothes. "All those girls! I bet they would love to have my collection of Eighties prom dresses!"

And they would, of course.

We can't say no. Some people have *good* clutter. One lady has been outfitting the girls for over a decade in last season's fashions. Then there are my tomato neighbors. We consume at least two

55

bumper crops each summer. We recently hit it big with a complete twin bed in great shape, allowing us to junk our youngest's previous charity bed. Yeah, it pays to keep an open van about it.

Sorting the helpful, the handy, and the hideous — it's a living.

Greg and I furnished our first apartment that way, you know. We lived in an upscale neighborhood in Austria where people left BMWs out by the curb when they got tired of them. One garbage night we decided to cash in. We went out and cased the neighborhood, returning in triumph with a dish rack and a long hallway rug that looked as if it had only been used outdoors for about five years. But it was free!

It's been twenty years, but my husband still remembers that lean era as if it were yesterday. In fact, he remembers it as if it were today.

Greg's inner miser comes out to gripe every time one of the kids spills something. "Don't use the paper towels!" he cries. "Go get a rag. Geez, these kids are always wasting things! Look at that, a perfectly good paper towel, and she wipes up the floor with it!"

Where he got the idea that paper towels are merely decorative . . . I'm gonna have to stop buying the ones with flowers on them.

Me? I take after my mother. She had the garbage-picking gene, but I never knew until one of my brothers started having children. At about that same time, the neighbor kids across the street outgrew a series of chunky, colorful toys that, like their kids, got progressively bigger and bolder: a doll stroller, a red wagon, a bicycle. My mom shamelessly retrieved these things in broad daylight.

One time they deposited something heavy — I think it was a Mercedes — by the curb, and she asked another of my brothers to go and get it. Like a dutiful son he did not let on how mortified he was. He put on a trench coat, pulled his hat down over his eyes, and waited until dark.

Handouts and Hand-Me-Downs

My mother's appreciation for fine freebies was a revelation. It explained why I went through childhood with one hand sticking out.

At about age seven or eight, my best friend and I went door-to-door to raise money to support our candy habit. But we didn't expect something for absolutely nothing. We were going to sing for our supper.

We knocked on an old lady's door, figuring she'd love a visit from two sweet things like us. Then we commenced wowing her:

> *Comet, it makes your teeth turn green.*
> *Comet, it tastes like gasoline.*
> *Comet, it makes you vomit,*

And the big finish:

> *So get your Comet and vomit today!*

We stepped forward, handed her a dandelion, and waited.

Oddly enough, she didn't produce cash. She mumbled, "Thank you," then slowly faded back into the recesses of her lonely house. We never saw her door open again.

So we came up with a better plan. We would go door-to-door selling a product. Luckily the market for painted rocks was wide open.

This was more successful. One neighbor in particular, a kind elderly gentleman, was good for a nickel apiece. We bragged to our friends, who, smelling the money, began to give us competition. One kid even went so far as to try to sell my mother a bundle of sticks tied with a string. When I heard his sales pitch — "You can put it in your house for a decoration" — I quit worrying. What a moron! Who the heck would decorate with a bundle of sticks when they could have *rocks*?

The rocks scheme dried up when we noticed that the neighbor man was decorating the underside of his shrubbery with them. This brought us face-to-face with one of the harsh realities of life: people just don't want decorative rocks. I tried telling that to the guys at Home Depot, but they wouldn't listen. They just kept piling decorative rocks higher and higher next to the bundles of sticks. Losers!

In our teens, another friend and I hit upon a scheme that couldn't miss. Indeed, selling homemade chocolate-chip cookies to our neighbors was a hot business. We spent hours baking these generous-size cookies, wrapped them up while still warm, and watched them sell like the hotcakes they were for fifty cents a half-dozen. My friend's mother humored us the first couple of times, probably glad we weren't out smoking. But after two of these episodes, she sat us down to teach us a little lesson in economics. She calculated the cost of all the ingredients — her ingredients — and then robbed us of our booty. When she was done with us, we had approximately two nickels to rub together. Enough to go into a rock-painting business.

What did this teach us? That mothers are a big pain in the rear!

No, really — it was a teachable moment. We learned that it was time to grow up. People were not going to indulge our rocks or cookie business anymore. It had gotten old. We had gotten old. It was time to mature. Time to put away the things of childhood.

So after that we started smoking.

But have no fear. It didn't last. We simply couldn't afford it.

∞

A Penny Saved Is a Frizzy Perm

I do home haircuts.

This is something I got from my father. When my brothers were little, my father figured he's save a few bucks by investing in some electric buzzers. By the time we girls were born, the gadget had paid for itself — but then, he must have thought, why waste the surplus money to engage the services of someone who'd actually been trained to cut hair? That wouldn't have been consistent with our do-it-yourself lifestyle.

I have several pictures of myself in Pop's barber chair, grinning. He is sitting behind me, holding his buzzer and also grinning. "Hey!" we seem to be saying, "isn't this *Reichswehr*-helmet hairstyle adorable?"

Such positive experiences with home thrift naturally made me wish to follow in my father's goose steps. Like an army on the march, the New England thrift gene is a force to be reckoned with. It can instantly multiply the cost of hair maintenance by the number of children — factoring in tips and mileage to the hairdresser's.

Is it worth it? I mean, such professionals will not make you look like a Nazi, but sometimes they act like one themselves. I had one who used to stick her fingers in my ears, wiggle them up and down, and holler, "Sit schtill! I am giving zee orders here!"

Then there is the R-rated conversation — words such as *done* and *fixed* are often in the script, and they do not refer to hair. "Sorry kids, no one under seventeen admitted without a guardian. Now sit down here on my professional toilet lid and pick a hairstyle. What'll it be? I can do *Reichswehr*, spaghetti string, and Emo."

Lest you think I started learning the craft on my helpless children, know that I had done a brief apprenticeship on my husband when we were first married. I had one style in my repertoire: the salad-bowl special. Greg's indelible handsomeness made me believe I had talent. But his hair was nothing like the stuff our daughters got.

Why does God do that? I mean, for the good of the species, I had married a man with the kind of hair you could name a candy bar after: *Rich Dark Chocolate Wave*. But did it matter? The kids took after me, Rollercoaster Head: precariously up, straight down, sudden turns. At times you wanted to cover your eyes and scream. Luckily they were cute, so there was a limit to the damage I could cause. Besides, I could always pretend they had gotten into the blunt-nosed scissors and cut it themselves.

Now, toddlers are not picky about haircuts. Their only criterion for a good haircut is that it doesn't take too long. They are very vocal about delays — which they blame entirely on me.

After about one minute they start squirming. I try to warn them: "Careful, Sweetie. You'd look funny in mismatched ears." But they insist that they're holding still. They tell me they are only wiggling their feet, which are nowhere near their heads. I try to explain that an earthquake in the feet sends aftershock tremors up to the head. This does not work.

I don't have the expertise to keep them still. Only professional hairdressers do. They have a secret incantation given to them with blood oath on the day they receive their licenses. It enables them to cut children's hair with precision, leaving their ears attached, and all the while smiling and exchanging fond compliments with them.

I have only, "See the splotch on the bathroom mirror? Glue your eyes to that."

"Are we almost done???"

"Yes," I say, squinting into their faces and bringing the ends down to the chin the way I'd seen professionals do. "I just have to check if it's even."

"Again?"

No fond compliments are exchanged. In fact, we had one child who, at the mere sight of the scissors, would throw open the windows and scream, "Child abuse! Call 911!"

Yet I persevered. It took me about ten years of practice, so don't take it as bragging when I say that I can now cut straight. Meanwhile, my children are collaborating on a tell-all memoir: *Mommy Scissorhands*.

I don't blame them. I had a history with my mother as well.

Her specialty was home perms. I was twelve when Mom gave me my first one. I'd gone AWOL from my father's chair in favor of the spaghetti-string look. Every night, Mom would go at it with a rattail comb, picking out any number of twigs and assorted greens I'd acquired from climbing trees and falling out of them. Once she extracted a cherry. During the winter my hair was cleaner, but a magnet for static. Half stuck to my head while the rest of it floated away from my face. I should have entered my head in the school science fair.

So one day Mom said, "I know just what you need: a perm!" She thought a perm would make my hair submit and behave on a regular basis — something she'd been trying to get me to do for quite some time. We went to the drug store. "Here's a good one," she said, holding up a box. *"Frizz: For kinks and knots without the twigs and cherries.* And it's on sale!"

Mom believed in using the smallest rollers available. The tighter the curls, the longer they would last. We soon ran out of those and went to the next size, then the next. In the end I had a rainbow of curlers in various sizes dispersed randomly around my scalp. Then there was the problem of wrapping. If you don't tuck in the ends just right, your head comes out looking like a pompom. (This is the real reason professional perms are so expensive. You are paying for experience.)

Timing, however, was the finishing touch. Here, mom parted ways with the directions, always afraid the perm wouldn't take. "Let's see, it says twenty minutes, but your hair is so fine that we'll leave it on for an extra fifteen. That will make *sure* it sets." The outcome of this tale isn't pretty. You've heard of the Dorothy Hamill, the Princess Di? I sported the Bozo the Clown.

From that day on, I was addicted to perms. (They say that people who grow up in permed households are twice as likely to get addicted to perms themselves.) I let my mom give me another, and another, and another — the classic definition of insanity. I firmly believed that no one with fine, straight hair such as mine could be expected to live with it. It was one of the effects of Original Sin and required constant mortification.

A few years later, Mom quit. She put away her wrapping papers, donated her rods to the blind, and took me to her hairdresser. But she never became fully rehabilitated. Every time I walked out the door headed for the hairdresser, she would shout, "Get her to do it really *tight* this time so it will last!"

But today I'm happy to announce that I've been a recovering permaholic since 1993. My hair is finally free to hang loose and be itself. Its cost and maintenance are minimal. And it looks remarkably normal.

Meanwhile the older girls appear to have inherited a generous share of their dad's indelible handsomeness. Or maybe it's just that they learned to book their own haircuts. The younger girls look sweet now that I've mastered layering. So all that's left is the boy.

Not a problem. My dad just gave me his extra buzzers.

∞

Feast Your Eyes, Not Your Face

Don't get my family started on food. I mean that literally. Don't get them started eating because they don't know when to stop.

If you mention the subject of food at our house, you're in for a riot the likes of which hasn't been seen since the Bolsheviks took over. There is always some crisis. It doesn't matter how much I buy, there is never enough food in the house. The way the kids stand in front of the fridge at lunchtime, you'd think they'd gotten up at four in the morning and stood in a bread line until noon only to find a sign in the fridge that says, "Have a grape?"

They blame me, of course. They refuse to acknowledge their part in the shortages.

The way I see it, after I get home from a $500 shopping run, lug in the grocery bags, and put it all away, the thing to do is to let the food alone for a while — let it get used to its new environment. It must be scary, being surrounded by nine people looking at you intensely as if they want to do away with you. That's a lot of pressure. Just leave it alone! Turn off the pantry light, and close the door. Let it get comfortable, and maybe it will reproduce.

But no. Everybody dives on it as if they haven't seen food for days.

Bless Me, Father, for I Have Kids

Yes, they had been complaining that we were "out of food." But by "food" they meant chips and frozen pizza. I'd been telling them for days that there was plenty of oatmeal and that I did spy a few raisins in the back corner of the pantry. What about all those bouillon cubes? Add a few kernels of rice, and you have soup. Stop being so picky, for heaven's sake.

They prefer more satisfying (read: convenient) food. Take hamburger pickles. It says right on the label that they are meant for — anyone? *Hamburgers.* With my kids, it's open jar, insert fork, and commence eating — no hamburgers in sight. Yet the label does not say, "Try as a substitute for potato chips." They eat sliced American cheese the same way. Everyone knows that sliced American cheese is meant to be surrounded by ham and bread — and accessorized with a pickle if you can find one.

At least that's what I recall from *my* eating days. Since becoming a mother I have learned to live without food. My motor runs mainly on coffee. I'm a hybrid. I don't need expensive fuel. I'm a highly developed machine — part human, part mother. All I need to do to feel satisfied is watch my baby eat.

Lately my baby hasn't been cooperating. He's at that stage where you set him down in the high chair and you give him something he loves, such as a grape, and he grins gleefully, looks at you adoringly, and hurls it at your face. Once he discovered his pitching arm, everything became a missile — carrots, bread, chips, spaghetti, and wet, salty hamburger pickles.

Back in the years B.C. (Before Children), when I was waitressing, the high-chair zone was the biggest challenge. Cleaning up a high-chair zone was like trying to vacuum a beach at low tide. Petrified bread rocks, chunks of animal parts strewn about, and plenty of sand on the carpet. On the tray there was enough liquid to go wading. Hungry seagulls circled overhead. As I wiped and vacuumed up this edible biome, I used to wonder if indeed it had sustained life that day. Did anything go *into* the child?

True mothers cannot eat under these conditions. If Solomon were alive today and he wanted to do a maternity test, he wouldn't have to resort to drastic measures. All he would have to do is watch them at feeding time. False Mother would sit there, calmly eating the last of the spaghetti, trying not to lose her appetite by looking over at the pasty high chair, ignoring the grape missiles being lobbed at her head. True Mother would be sitting with her back to the table, bravely leaning over the gunky high chair while pleading, "Fine! If you won't eat Mommy's good food, how about a potato chip? Yum — it's dusted in chemically altered spices, and I got it away from the teens just for you, my sweet! No? How about yesterday's Cheerios? Wee Debris forgot to wipe your seat yesterday and I found them underneath the cushion. [Sigh.] Okay, how about something off the floor?"

Such a sacrificial ritual goes on in our house every lunch hour. Meanwhile the other kids sulk in front of their raisins and bouillon, whining, "How come *he* gets the spaghetti?"

They're sure that I'm starving them on his behalf. If dinner happens to be something he likes, there is no chance of seconds. I grab whatever's left in the pot, spoon it into a plastic container, and label it "Joey's lunch tomorrow" with a skull and crossbones underneath. I can't help it if whatever he likes, they happen to like too. It's not as if I'm keeping them from foods they'd gladly give up for Lent, such as spinach. It's the creamy pastas and rices, the freshly cut watermelon, and the muffins I squirrel away.

This is a matter of survival. Not just his, mine. Watching Joey during those rare moments when he actually does eat — he can put it away like a bear before hibernation — acts like an appetizer on me. My digestive juices begin to flow. All clear for Mom to eat!

Bless Me, Father, for I Have Kids

Let's celebrate! Pass the bouillon! Joey's had enough. He will live a few more days!

Meanwhile, the rest of the family refuses to be satisfied along with me. I know where they get these uncooperative habits — from my husband. He's been complaining of an involuntary hunger strike since we've been married.

Every morning he appears at breakfast fed up — not literally — and says, "Why is there nothing on the table for me?"

To be fair, he has been working for two hours before breakfast. Now he has an appetite for the Number Five special at The Greasy Spoon Diner: a slab of bacon, two eggs, hash browns, and wheat toast with a side of fried onions. He'd like it even better to have this served by somebody who calls him "hon" and whose only job of the morning is to make him happy.

I try to compromise. "Here's some coffee . . . hon." Then I point out our expansive menu. "Sara Lee has gotten up early, and today we have some freshly baked blueberry muffins."

Huns do not eat girlie food. "That couldn't keep a cat alive."

Figures the toughest customers are the regulars. "Okay, what'll you have, hon?"

"Food!" he answers.

"Could you be more specific?"

"FOOD!"

I know that the customer is always right, but he's not paying me enough to stand there and guess what he wants for breakfast. "All right," I say, "I'll tell you what's available. There's yogurt."

"Yes!"

"There's oatmeal."

"Yes!"

"And egg."

"Any bacon?"

"No."

"Well, I take the eggs."

"*Egg*. After Sara baked the blueberry muffins, there's only one left."

"Look," he says. "I'll just take the spaghetti from last night. I'm starving."

I hesitate.

"Let me guess," he says, sighing. "Joey's lunch? Okay, but don't expect a tip."

What Greg and the girls fail to realize is that Joey is actually not part of the problem. He is the solution. If the others really want to make me go out and buy their version of food, all they have to do is convince Joey to drink up the milk. I will then put aside all other tasks of the day and run to the store to get more for him. While I am getting milk, it is highly likely that I will throw a few hundred other staples into the cart: pickles, potato chips, frozen pizza, and some luxuries as well, such as bacon and eggs.

And coffee. Can't forget that. I have to survive too.

∞

Please Overlook the Following Qualifications

Recent articles in women's magazines show a definite change in trend: the decades of calling homemakers "unemployed" are over. According to one such article, in fact, homemaking teaches valuable skills that would look great on a resume. For instance, conflict resolution (who gets the last slice of pizza — the kid who called it first or the kid who ate half of it when no one was looking?), relevant life experience (wipes runny noses; picks gum from sneakers; removes sand from bathing suits), and budgeting skills (can feed nine people on income for four). Best of all, the article stated, is organization. Modern moms know how to manage all kinds of tasks virtually at the same time.

Yes, that's true to a point. I can easily take someone to the potty, give a spelling quiz, and answer the phone all while burning dinner.

But I doubt such home organizational skills would transfer easily to an office setting. I've always known I wasn't cut out for office work. My mom, a former secretary with advanced filing and typing skills plus impeccable penmanship, had hoped otherwise. So at some point in my teens she suggested I get trained as a medical secretary.

I couldn't see it. At the time, my filing system consisted of shoving stuff (shoes, socks, my homework) under my bed. Today, twenty-plus years later, I've made progress. I still shove stuff under my bed — mainly socks — but usually not important papers. Those go into piles placed carefully around the house.

The main pile is in the "mail basket," which brims over with pizza coupons, magazines, kids' drawings, letters, wedding invitations, unpaid bills, odd bits of jewelry, and socks waiting to be shoved under the bed. I keep telling the kids not to put mail in there, but they forget.

Another important pile is on the cabinet under the microwave. It contains tablecloths, pizza coupons, recipe books, letters, bills, phone books, socks, and unpaid church envelopes.

The really, really important pile is on my desk. That's where I keep all the things I am supposed to be attending to immediately: bills, the registration form for my child's high school diploma program, applications for free membership in warehouse shopping, notes on my writing assignments, the baby's outgrown shoes, computer CDs, and socks. When that pile gets out of hand, I shove it into a drawer. (The socks are happy.) When the drawers fill up — well, I revert to under the bed. On my resume, that skill is called: *Ability to file outside of the box.*

The problem is that important papers don't always fit into the standard file box. Don't you just hate those people who use gigantic long paper? "Hello, mortgage lender — 8.5 x 14-size paper is not standard. What's with the extra three inches? Do you know how hard it is to shove something that size under a bed?"

Everyone in the Real World knows that 8.5 x 11 is standard. That is what I use: clean, white, one-sided scrap paper. I use it mainly if math is required — such as figuring out where we are going to get a spare $10,000 to put toward our child's college tuition.

Please Overlook the Following Qualifications

This paper is filed in various places around the house, mainly under socks. All other important information goes on the backs of envelopes — such as the phone number of the really kindhearted bank in India that will give me that ten grand I need, if I would be a dear and first wire them five grand to cover expenses.

When I really have something important to remember, however, I don't take any chances. I use sticky notes. Sticky notes can be stuck at eye level in places I am most likely to notice them: the

refrigerator, the stove hood, and the bathroom mirror. Sticky notes remind me which important papers I will need to retrieve for certain tasks.

Now, you are probably wondering how my file retrieval system works. I'm glad you asked. When it comes time to find something, my method has three parts. First, I pick through the odd-sock basket unsuccessfully. Then I walk around the house, yelling, "WHO moved my stuff? I'M GONNA KILL SOMEBODY!" After that I dump out the various baskets, throw things out of the cabinet, and sweep all the papers off my desk onto the floor.

Bingo! Two weeks later the paper turns up. It was downstairs in the basement on top of the play kitchen set. (The basement is where the kids file important papers. They refuse to learn.) That's when I remember, *Oh yeah, this paper was on the dining-room table, surrounded by toys.*

I told the kids to clear the table for supper, and they put the paper downstairs with the toys. Why didn't I think of that before?

And my mother thought I should have power over life and death.

"Excuse me, Mr. Smith, take a seat in the waiting room while I look for your file. All right, WHO moved Mr. Smith's file? I'M GONNA KILL SOMEONE! SOMEBODY IS GONNA DIE!

"Oh no, not you, Mr. Smith; I sincerely hope it doesn't come to that. I've been lucky so far. Ten years at this job and nobody has died. It's been close a few times . . . WHY CAN'T I EVER FIND ANYTHING? NOTHING IS WHERE I LEFT IT!

"Wait a minute, Mr. Smith. I know — where were you examined the last time you were here? Room C? Bingo! I remember now; I left your file on top of the magazines in Room C. Then we put the magazines out for recycling, so I moved your file to the top of the green recycling bin. When were you here last? Six months ago? Hmmm, it hasn't turned up. My guess is it fell in with the recycling. Sorry, that information is no longer available. Tell you what, let's start over. What was your trouble again? Anxiety attacks? Hold on, let me get a bigger sticky note."

∞

Don't Poke the Big Cat

There is a Youtube video called "Never Poke a Big Cat," in which a park ranger tries to get a wildcat out of a cage by poking her with a stick. The wildcat comes out of the cage all right, and attacks the ranger through his open jeep window.

My sympathies are with the cat. Here she is, alone in her room for once, catching a cat nap between pressing household duties, and this ranger shows up and jabs her. Typical man — I know what he's thinking. "You don't *look* busy. Come on, quit lazing around. I've got a schedule to keep. You can sleep later." And she's thinking, "Oh sure, have *you* ever tried to sleep in the wild? Monkeys chattering nonstop, elephants charging up and down the plains, and the last time I found a cozy upper limb to hang out on, there was a tsetse fly in it."

The ranger pokes her again. She growls, "If you poke me one more time, young man, I'll chew that arm off."

But does he listen? Finally, she pokes back — with her teeth. And when it's all over, the sympathy goes to the ranger. People are rallying around him, he's rubbing what's left of his arm, and everybody blames the cat, thinking, "Geesh! Keep that dart gun handy, Sahib."

They then put the cat back into the cage, which is where she wanted to be all along. She rolls her eyes.

Poking is a sure sign of an underdeveloped brain. It's something children do. You can't hold it against them; they don't know better.

My kids are fast learners, though. They each try it exactly once. I simply bare my fangs, and they get the message.

Thereafter I trained each and every one of them to get my attention the way a rational adult would: leave a message on my answering machine, and I'll get back to you in three or four days. Whatever you do, don't put your hands on me unless authorized. Any poking, tapping, or yanking on my clothing constitutes provocation before the law of the jungle.

They have one or two friends who don't know this about me. These kids remind me of certain dogs who automatically leap upon persons least likely to appreciate slobber on their faces. Not long ago, I dropped my daughter off to babysit, and the family border collie (motto: "Hop until you drop") bypassed our daughter (motto: "I've never kissed a dog I didn't like") to spring up into my face. He then started the get-to-know-you game up my skirt.

Some of my children's friends have shown affection in similarly antagonizing ways. They've tackled me until the wind was knocked out of me, made me gag from an assaulted Adam's apple, and knocked the knees right out from under me. Recovery from such hugs takes a couple of days, so I've had plenty of time to smile at them while blood and breath slowly seeps back in, to say, "Thank you, dear. I love you too."

Then there's that measured-thrust-of-a-finger-poke-in-my-arm, or, if you really want to see some fireworks, my side. Luckily God knew I was potentially volatile, so He wired my detonator with a slow-burning fuse. Within five seconds to blast, my children know to spring from their chairs, usher the poker to a safe distance, and shriek, "Don't poke the big cat!"

You know how some dog owners have invisible fences that zap them if they stray? Well, I have a force field. People who violate it without permission are in danger of electrocution. In my house, everybody is supposed to recognize my force field. My two oldest teens have developed one too, only they call it a bubble. My husband calls it "being a Yankee."

It doesn't matter what you call it; just don't poke it, tap it, sniff it, kick its chair, or in the case of a wayward boy trying to get attention from one of the girls, rest your leg on it. It is sacred. It is dangerous. Picture the fate of the Nazis who opened the Ark of the Covenant in *Raiders of the Lost Ark*.

The same thing goes for the bedroom. My boudoir is open by invitation only. Our kids are welcome, of course. And by special arrangement, my husband. Once in awhile I invite my girlfriends in to chat, show them the decor, or look at something on the computer. My children's friends, as well as any adult men who haven't been hired to fix the wiring or shampoo the rug, are *verboten*.

Just last week I was typing away in the sanctuary, and I heard a knock on my door. Before I could turn around, it opened and I heard a high, squeaky voice say:

"Mithith Lloyd?"

It was the voice of Pushie, our eleven-year-old's guest — the same shy, lisping child who left twelve phone messages for our daughter when we were away at the beach for a week last June: "Why don't you call me back?! [*Gasp, gasp!*] I'm thort of breath. I can't thleep! I'm going on a hunger thtrike until you call! I need you! [*Choke, gurgle.*]"

I turned around slowly. Not one of my children was nearby to perform a rescue. Something took possession of me. I heard myself speaking in a voice my sister used once to play Dracula in a garage spook show:

"You entered the sanctorium. You can *not do that.*"

She stared at me with big round eyes.

Suddenly I imagined myself locked away in state prison (with a stake through my heart). *What am I doing? She's just a little girl. What if she tells her mother that she had to grab the crucifix off the wall to defend herself?!*

I quickly explained about the rules of closed doors and what if I was sleeping, getting dressed, nursing the baby, etc.? "I'm not mad at you, dear," I said, adding lying to my list of sins. "I tell my own children these things." I spied my daughter hiding in the shadows. "Don't I?" From well out of range, she nodded. I smiled at Pushie nervously.

"Okay . . ." she replied. "I was jutht wondering if you have any thnacks. I looked through the cupboard, and I didn't thee anything."

My daughter grabbed her, ushered her to a safe distance, and quickly shut my door.

It was either that or a dart gun.

∞

A Lesson from St. Paul's Letter to the Husbands
(the PMS Translation)

One of the biggest disputes in the Church today is over the roles of the sexes. This is not just a problem at the Vatican. It trickles down to home life. To illustrate, please note the following syllogisms.

I.

St. Paul says women should cover their heads in church.

Susie is a woman.

Therefore, Greg has just proven that Susie should cover her head in church.

II.

Susie has nothing personal against St. Paul — except that he is a guy.

Susie is not a guy.

Therefore, Susie does not believe that not wearing a hat in church will send her to purgatory until the end of time — if she is lucky.

Greg would say the second one is a false syllogism. To which I quote St. Hildehair of Barehead on the subject: "Yeah, but no one else is wearing one."

Besides this appeal to trusty authority, I have several arguments to back myself up, possibly even against a wall.

Argument Number One:
Decent headgear is not found in stores.

These days even baby bonnets are hard to get hold of. Trust me, I've tried. Other than baseball caps, men's straw hats, and ski hats, your friendly neighborhood Humongomart does not carry headwear.

Upscale stores do carry dressy hats made of felt, in various colors and bedecked with a feather or jewel. Greg thinks these are beautiful. Such hats are worn by people who also wear lace gloves and carry a scented handkerchief to go out and buy meat; for example, his grandmother in about 1947.

You may visit a thrift store and find — if lucky — several dozen vintage hats such as Greg's grandmother wore. Our teenage daughter has a collection of these hanging on her bedroom wall. It burns Greg up to see them there. "What's wrong with these?!" he exclaims. "Nothing," I tell him, "except it looks like somebody nuked a florist's. See the pink mushroom cloud?"

Other than the examples listed above, plus a few miscellaneous styles of hats as worn by teenagers and the odd dozen or so styles for women my age, there are no hats available. None!

Okay, my husband says. So why not wear a mantilla then?

Argument Number Two:
I put away the things of childhood.

I grew up wearing a mantilla, or the abridged version — a doily. My mother always wore a mantilla, and when I was a child

A Lesson from St. Paul's Letter to the Husbands

she insisted I cover my head also. With whatever was handy at the time, be it a knit hat with a pom-pom on the end, a parka hood, or my left hand.

At least she never tried pinning a tissue on top of my head. However, my self-image suffered. Rather than leaving me to ride anonymously on the conveyor belt to purgatory, the head covering outed me in front of my whole parochial-school class. Martyrdom ensued.

Years passed. I married Greg, in the confidence that he had not been raised like me. His mother's collection of doilies was kept underneath various lamps and vases and on the backs of easy chairs. Then one day he cracked open St. Paul, and I was cooked. In purgatory. No more indulgence for me.

Did you ever notice how guys can get together with other guys and puzzle over the difficult passages of St. Paul?

"Does Paul endorse predestination, or doesn't he?"

"Who was this man he speaks of who was caught up in the third heaven?"

"What precisely is meant by salvation through faith?"

But when it comes to the duties of women, the pages of St. Paul are black and white. "It says right here you have to cover your head," say guys, pointing. "While we're at it, a woman shorn is a disgrace, so cancel that haircut. Don't try to get out of it because" — *flip, flip, flip* — "you gotta obey me too. It says so right" — *flip* — "here."

Thereupon most women flip out. Which brings me to:

Argument Number Three:
St. Paul says, "See if you can make her."

St. Paul also talks about what a pain it is to deal with a wife and how it's just easier for those attending upon the Lord (priests) not to bother. Put succinctly, "Husbands: Bug your wives and pretty soon you may be celibate like me." (No, I am not planning to go into translating.)

Argument Number Four:
It's distracting.

I can vouch for this because I did wear a mantilla for the first ten years of my married life. St. Paul seemed to want me to, Greg definitely wanted me to, and back then I was still somewhat respectable. It was fine at Trad Masses, where, if you didn't do it, somebody might offer you a scented hanky to put over your head. (Disposable tissues, not existing prior to the Council of Trent, are frowned upon.) But at our regular parish — which is Ukrainian — I had a problem. Nobody complied except for a few ancient (and I am sure very holy) *babushkas*. Everyone else's head was uncovered. Not only that, but disgracefully shorn as well. As I and my daughters sat there, covered by various mantillas, hats, and bandanas, I couldn't get my mind off my head. I'd give it a sidelong glance, first right then left. I felt as if I had a UFO hovering over my head. Sometimes people would ask me about it. One guy even asked if I was Amish.

I got rid of the veil and downsized to a doily. Greg was not pleased. It was my own fault. If I had called the thing a "chaplet," it would have been okay. *Chaplet*: the word sounds much like *chapel*. But no. I had to up and nickname it a doily. Greg tolerated this compromise only because it was harder for the baby to yank off.

The girls soon followed me into doilydom. We used to fight about who got the black one, which wasn't as noticeable as the white ones. "That's it!" Greg announced one Sunday. "We are *not* wearing doilies!" (We had no time to retort, "Whaddya mean

A Lesson from St. Paul's Letter to the Husbands

we?") He grabbed a pile of lace lying in a heap in the dining room and brought it out to the car. "Here! *We* are wearing veils!"

"Excuse me, Dad, but, like, these are the dining-room curtains. Mom's getting ready to paint."

After that our eldest teen started wearing big sunglasses on her head at Mass. I was tempted to call her "bikini head" but remembered the doily fall-out and kept my mouth shut. I was not going to be a traitor. I know it was not patriarchal of me but then again, St. Paul expects me to be difficult. Wouldn't want to contradict him, now would we?

Who knows how it will all end? I have fought the good fight, and I continue to fight it. But I have kept the faith. If a crown awaits me, I sure hope everyone else is wearing one too. I wouldn't want to stick out.

∞

Holywood Squares

Ever wonder what life would be like if someday we got our dearest wish and our nation made an instant conversion to the Faith? In times past, when a nation received Christianity, it could still take hundreds of years for the culture to catch up. The mystic must co-exist with the magician, the prioress with the priestess, and the sacraments with superstition. The pagan rites had a way of lingering in the air like the smell of burnt herring after a Lenten Friday meal.

If modern America were suddenly Christian, all TVs would require conversion boxes. What sort of product would the culture of materialism and mindless entertainment make if suddenly all its references were Catholic? Would we have, for instance, Catholic Reality TV?

You've Got a Secret: We've installed a hidden camera inside Fr. O'Gruffy's confessional. Uh oh — don't look now, but here comes Mrs. Klempchik. In last month's confession, she confessed comparing her boss to something a vulture would eat. What will she say this time? Tune in tomorrow. And as always, YOU give the penance. Will it be three Hail Marys, one random act of kindness, or fifty flagellations? Call in with your vote: 1 888 WE GOT YA.

What would become of steamy soap-opera scenes?

Luke: Laura, I need you. You're my life!

Laura: For shame! You forget I'm married to Scotty. Then again, maybe I could dump him and get an annulment.

No? Perhaps those things *would* be phased out rather quickly. But I can see no reason to nix good clean entertainment. Take game shows. If we could just steer them away from crass materialism, with a little help from above . . .

It's time for the Holywood Squares! The game where squares compete to get to heaven.

Voice from Above: One of these saints is sitting in the secret square and the aspirant who picks it first could win a prize package worth up to four thousand days of perfect sinless indulgence!

Which saint is it? (*Continuous drum roll.*)
The honorable St. Matthew
The lovely St. Catherine of Siena
The venerable St. Teresa of Avila
Mr. G. K. Chesterton
The jocular St. Philip Neri
TV star Archbishop Fulton J. Sheen
Pope John Paul II
The Mystifying Blessed Anna Maria Taigi
Or the formidable St. Paul!
. . . all on the Holywood Squares.
And here's the master of the Holywood Squares: St. Peter! (*Wild applause.*)

St. Peter: Thank you and welcome. Hello, Saints!

Saints: Hello, St. Peter!

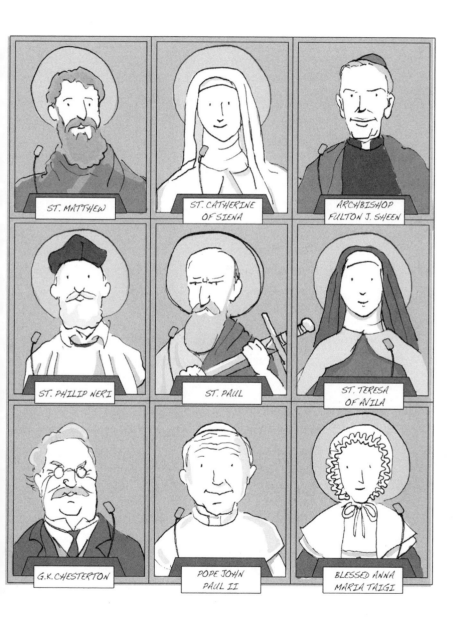

Bless Me, Father, for I Have Kids

St. Peter: A godly group this evening. All right. Let's start with the *alpha* and *omega*, the O symbol. Over on this side we have Mrs. Mary Prairie of Wichita, Kansas. Mary is a housewife and mother of ten. She recently launched her own line of modest fashions. Well, perhaps Blessed Anna will look you up?

Bl. Anna: Got any itchy plain wool?

Mary: That's my specialty.

St. Peter: And over here at the crosses, the X symbol, is Mrs. Rusty Beatupvan! Mrs. Beatupvan is a veteran homeschooling mom. She and her husband have six children and five on the way. Did I read that right? You have five on the way?

Rusty: Yes, that's right, Peter. We hope I can win enough grace tonight to bring them home from that orphanage in China.

St. Peter: Well, good luck to you both — although I don't really believe in luck. Remember, aspirants: the first aspirant to pick the secret square could win a brand-new fiery chariot! (*Applause.*) Mary, we start with you.

Mary: I'll take St. Catherine of Siena.

St. Peter: St. Catherine, the inventor of which invention won the No-hell Peace Prize for the twentieth century?

St. Catherine: My mother would say it was the playpen. Twenty-six children, you know! (*Laughter.*) No, seriously.

It was the digital camera. When it's six-hundred-plus years after your death and people are still photographing you, you want that nifty enhanced-lighting feature. Gives your complexion a healthy glow.

St. Peter: Mary?

Mary: I agree.

St. Peter: Actually it was the Girl Scout cookie. These things are delivered right to your door. Busy moms depend on them. They're even producing a documentary about it: A Convenient Tooth. Sweet!

Rusty: St. Matthew, please.

St. Peter: St. Matthew, what number would you have to divide the number of Sunday communicants by to get the number of those at Saturday Confession?

St. Matthew: (*stroking his beard*) Gee, I could tell you the tax code of Palestine circa AD 30 . . . Hmmm . . . I'll go with — this is just a look through a dark glass — 144,000.

St. Peter: Rusty?

Rusty: I'll disagree.

St. Peter: No, sorry, Rusty. That is correct. It's Mary's turn.

Mary: St. Teresa of Avila?

St. Peter: St. Teresa, what is the proper way to dispose of a ratty scapular?

St. Teresa: Well, we never had that problem with ours. They're too big and bunchy. Um, but I think it's either burial or cremation.

Mary: I agree!

St. Peter: Actually, you just send them to that great big bag of broken rosaries in the sky. Put them on a shelf or in a drawer, and let them pile up until the Second Coming. Rusty?

Rusty: St. Philip Neri.

St. Peter: St. Philip, how did God respond to Cain when Cain cockily asked, "Am I my brother's keeper?"

St. Philip: Um, "Not anymore"?

St. Peter: You're going to go with that?

St. Philip: I have inside information . . .

Rusty: I disagree.

St. Peter: Good going, Rusty!

St. Philip: Wait a minute, Rusty. That's what your eight-year-old wrote on his religion test, and you didn't mark it wrong.

St. Peter: Uh — Mary?

Mary: I'll take G. K. Chesterton.

Bells and whistles go off.

St. Peter: You've just picked the Secret Square!

Mary starts jumping up and down.

St. Peter: If you get this right, you could win a brand-new fiery chariot! (*Applause.*) G. K. Chesterton, there's a lot rolling on this.

Chesterton: Well, I've been called "roly" before. (*Laughter.*)

St. Peter: What is the last line of this poem?
"As I was going to St. Fred's
I asked a kid to count the heads
Nine there were in chapel veils
Four wore hats, one a tail
Six were bald and shone like Windex . . ."

Chesterton: (*wincing*) Who wrote that? Shaw? Could I hear it again in Latin?

St. Peter: Sorry, it's not available in Latin. Unfortunately there's no word in Latin for Windex. Would you like me to read it again in English?

Chesterton: No! And don't call it English. Uh . . .
"Six were bald and shone like Windex
. . . One had on a sheet of Kleenex."

Mary: I'll agree.

St. Peter: Correct! Congratulations, Mary! (*Applause.*) Rusty, you still have a chance to win enough grace to adopt those kids. Pick a square.

Rusty: Servant of God, Bishop Sheen.

St. Peter: Bishop Sheen, the Cathedral in Aachen, Germany, is a popular pilgrimage destination. It holds an unusual relic. What is it?

Sheen: Oh yes, I've been there. The lovely young lady said they were the pampers of our Lord.

Rusty: I'll agree.

St. Peter: No. Actually, it's the swaddling clothes of our Lord. Wait — the judges say they'll accept your answer. "Pampers" is indeed what tour guides tell visiting Americans.

Sheen: They're in a gold reliquary shaped like a Diaper Genie.

St. Peter: Mary, you're up.

Mary: Holy Father, Pope John Paul II.

Thunderous applause. Photographers from L'Osservatore Romano *snap pictures. Somebody shouts:* Viva il Papa!

JP II: Woo-woo!

St. Peter: If only I had been pope in the communication age . . . sigh. Holy Father, or rather, Holy Successor, you are famous for many sayings. Scholars have sifted your writings and written volumes on your thought. Tell us, what is the meaning of *woo-woo*?

JP II: Be afraid. Be very afraid.

Mary: I'll disagree.

St. Peter: That was not an actual question. Just a little light humor, Mary. The actual meaning of *woo-woo* is unknown.

JP II: Even I don't know it.

St. Peter: One of life's great mysteries. Here's the question: What do St. Charles Lwanga, St. Eustatius, and St. Daniel all have in common?

JP II: The first name: *Saint*.

Mary: I'll agree.

St. Peter: Actually, it's their last name: *And Companions!* Rusty, one more X and you will win the game.

Rusty: I'd like Blessed Anna Maria Taigi.

St. Peter: Blessed Anna, what is the meaning of: *Audi filia et vide et inclina aurem tuam?*

Bl. Anna: Oh yes. I used to say it to my children every day. "Hearken, O daughter, and see, and incline thy ear." Psalm 44:11.

Rusty: I agree!

St. Peter: Judges? No, according to the latest ICEL rendering, it's actually: "Listen up kids, or I'm gonna start screaming." Mary, it's up to you now.

Mary: I'd like St. Paul.

St. Peter: St. Paul, does the Church have an official position on short hair on women? If so, what is it?

St. Paul: Beloved, in my day, short hair on girls was next door to being a Skinhead.

Rusty: I'll disagree with that!

St. Peter: Uh, Paul, put down the sword.

St. Paul: Who authorized you to speak, young lady?

St. Peter: I'll settle this. Rusty, it's not your turn. Mary?

Mary: I'll agree! And pants are bad too!

Blaring sound.

St. Peter: Well, that's the last trumpet. It means the time is up. Rusty, Mary, you've both been great. Mary, you've got those hot wheels. (*Applause.*) Rusty, you were so close to winning four thousand days of indulgence. But you did win enough grace to adopt those kids. Everybody give her a great big round of applause!

∞

The Uninterrupted Life
Is Not Worth Living

∽

What Kind of Homeschooler
Would You Be?
A Survey

There is no one right way to homeschool. Whichever method we choose, we know we can count on help from above. Answer these questions to find out which method would suit you best. Then check your answers to find out who your patron saint would be!

1. How would you define the word *basics*?
   A. The trivium and quadrivium.
   B. Reading, writing, arithmetic, religion, penmanship, great Western literature, spelling, Latin, vocabulary, art, music, history, science, at least two years of a modern foreign language, with labs, collages, and community service sprinkled throughout. But we're flexible. Take all the time you need. Lots of people graduate when they're twenty-four.
   C. A favorite pair of jeans. You can wear them to Mass or the mall or just for doing mock naval battles in your bathtub at home.

2. What does the word *classic* mean to you?
   A. Something that has stood the test of time, is relevant for every generation, and on which the very structure of all that is true, good, and beautiful rests.
   B. Vintage movies that don't have "stuff" in them. These include *Bedtime for Bonzo* and *A Man for All Seasons* — although you should be warned that the second one contains mature subject matter.
   C. A marketing word meaning "old unimproved formula." See "Coke."

3. What is your approach to grammar?
   A. Grammar is the foundation upon which all learning is laid; it immediately precedes the logic stage in the trivium.
   B. Grammar is the workbook in which fourth graders must underline the modifiers in sentences such as: "St. Geronimo was thrown from a steep parapet to the glee of the angry mob of his malicious persecutors."
   C. Grammar is boring, but we do know a few jokes in Latin: *Prehende uxorem meam, sis!* (Take my wife, please!)

4. Who is Cicero?
   A. Ancient Roman rhetorician, whose name means literally "chickpea." Cicero thought this was no reason to change his name, as another orator was called "fat ankles."
   B. Little-known Roman martyr, who converted after instigating the martyrdom of St. Geronimo. Please write a synonym for *instigating*.
   C. Owner of Cicero's Pizzeria, which has nifty maps of Italy on the walls.

5. Among neophytes, what is the most common objection to homeschooling as an educational alternative?
   A. What about socialization?
   B. How will he ever get into college without quantum transcalculus?
   C. We keep our neophytes in a tank and feed them twice a day. One got out once, and the dog ate him. We wrote it down as science.

6. What do you see as the biggest problem in modern education?
   A. It is anti-Western-civilization and bears the lion's share of blame for the dumbing-down of our society.
   B. It does not use enough big words, and it demonstrates abominable penmanship.
   C. Big Brother. You get in trouble just for losing a little paperwork or forgetting to show up for your hearing.

7. What do you look for in a curriculum?
   A. Must ever point to what is true.
   B. Has workbooks to keep you going through the flu.
   C. Uses large amounts of glue.

8. The Homeschool Fairy has granted you the help of any teacher of your choice. Who would your fantasy teacher be?
   A. St. Thomas Aquinas
   B. Sr. Mary Elephant
   C. The Homeschool Fairy

9. What is the hardest thing about homeschooling?
   A. Finding qualified tutors who can read the primary sources in their original languages.
   B. Finding time to instruct all ten children *and* cook *and* clean *and* teach NFP classes.

C. Finding the right-size Lego pieces to build a trebuchet to knock down our Lego medieval castle.

10. What is your attitude toward field trips?
    A. We are hoping to qualify for the Young Overachievers trip through Oxford University: *The Mystery of Stonehenge: Ancient Religious Beliefs and Superstition*.
    B. We would like to sign the children up for trips such as the one above; however, we can't afford to miss that many school days.
    C. Life is a field trip. By the way, "Stonehenge" by Spinal Tap is a really fun song.

Bonus question: How long do you plan to homeschool?
    A. Until the children demonstrate that their needs have grown beyond our resources, at which time they will simply enter college.
    B. Until death do us part.
    C. I do not understand this question. What do you mean by "plan"?

Check your answers to find your patron saint. If your answers were predominantly:

As: Your patron saint is St. Augustine of Hippo, best known for his brilliant masterpiece, *The City of God*.

Bs: Your patron saint is St. Augustine of Hippo, best known for leading a sinful life and then converting in spite of evil surroundings, due to the prayers of his long-suffering mother. (Please circle the modifiers.)

Cs: Your patron saint is St. Augustine of Hippo, best known for opening a random page of Scripture and instantly graduating from radical Manichean weirdo to brainy future bishop.

᠙

It's a Nerd! It's a Saint! It's Supermom!

Well, I don't know how it happened. There was a time when homeschoolers were doubted by the American public. "How do you do it all?!" the American public would exclaim with a horrified expression on its collective face. The implication was clear: "There is no way you can possibly do it. You should not even attempt to do it. You will fail at doing it."

But today, due to some sort of — well, voodoo, I suspect — the American public has changed its collective mind. It now thinks that homeschoolers can indeed do it, and do it well. All of it. We know because it exclaims, "How do you do it all?!" Only this time it is not wearing a horrified expression on its face. It is beaming with admiration.

Take a dear old lady at our church. She has done her civic duty and donated the genetic material required to produce two generations of Ivy League children. Yet she continues to tell me how amazing *I* am. One time she introduced me to her son, a cardiac surgeon, with the words, "This is Sue. She's so amazing. Look at all those lovely children. And she homeschools! Isn't she amazing?!" The man acted duly impressed. In his profession he is probably quite used to dealing graciously with inferiors.

Bless Me, Father, for I Have Kids

Granted, I was looking reasonably competent that morning after Mass. I stood there with my feet planted firmly on the carpet. I was not tipping over. I was not dragging toilet paper around under my shoe. Still, I failed to see the impressiveness of the situation. Her comments made me feel as if I were supposed to respond by performing some wonderful act, like call one of the kids over to recite the times tables. Or at least draw attention to the fact that none of them were spray-painting rude words on the wall. "Yes, yes," I could imagine the specialist saying, "very intelligent, well-behaved children. And look at you standing there. I dare say, you *do* look extremely competent this morning."

Instead I excused myself and went to hide under one of the pews.

Lord only knows what the dear lady — as fine a representative of the American public as I ever saw — thinks homeschoolers actually do. All I know is that she considers it impossible. I wish someone in the real world would let me know. I have only guesses.

Perhaps they picture a school scene in which a staff of dozens runs various operations — teaching, preparing hundreds of lunches, painting over graffiti. They wonder: How can a staff of one mother handle this? Is St. Isadore's guardian angel handling the chores?

"It's a miracle! A saint in our midst!"

I hate to erase the halo from the icon, especially because it's bound to leave a smudge in its place, but . . .

It ain't cardiac surgery — although a term from surgery does aptly describe it. *Triage* is how I get "everything" done. You know, if you've ever watched M*A*S*H, that triage is the evaluation and classification of wounded for purposes of treatment and evacuation. Granted, triage is used mainly in the midst of military bombardments or accident scenes involving multiple wounded parties. We have never technically had either of those (although

It's a Nerd! It's a Saint! It's Supermom!

now that we have a son, people keep telling us it's coming). Yet if you were to pick your way through the rubble of the girls' rooms, you might understandably look for shell fragments.

Their method for picking an outfit is to detonate their dressers and closet so that the clothes explode out all over the room. This textile fallout increases over time until it becomes necessary to sort, tag, and evacuate the critically dirty. Meanwhile tiny deadly landmines lurk in the rubble — such as cute glass figurines and sewing needles. Other useful household items have been swallowed up, never to be seen again.

These are the worst cases, of course. Yet even on an ordinary day, the rate of decay of an average family of nine makes triage the house cleaner's and homeschooler's method of choice.

Yes, triage makes it possible to have well-educated children, a decent home, and my morning coffee. On Sundays, when there is no homeschooling, I can even get my hair done.

Done? you say incredulously. Define *done*.

My hair takes a long time before it reaches doneness, yet very little actual labor is involved. It's kinda like baking bread: you know, how only four and a half minutes are spent actually laboring over it, and the rest you wait for the dough to rise? In my case, four and a half minutes are spent getting the hair to rise, and the rest waiting for it to droop. When it's at the right stage of droop, I simply spray it in place.

During the drooping period, the children are strictly forbidden to stampede, lest instant Matzoh-head occur.

You will agree that my method is preferable to the wash-and-shake method invented by the family dog.

Triage has also trained me to wait until I am in the car to get my face made up so that in-house time can be used more efficiently; for instance, to crawl around on the floor, sniffing out kids' missing shoes. This is not a problem on Sundays when Greg is driving. It's a bit tougher on weekdays when he's not. Fortunately we live in a densely populated area with plenty of traffic hangups.

The triage makeover coordinates perfectly with my wardrobe — which has been decorated just for me with stains by the children.

Introducing Haute Mama,
original fashions developed by kids.

On the Go   At Home   Enceinte

If it's not stained, it's not authentic.
Look for these designs in closets now!

Now, there is a certain breed of homeschooler who manages to balance home and school on a regular basis, and look put-together at all times, and drive around town slowly without applying mascara at the same time. I don't use the term *breed* accidentally, for they have many children and they are the purebreds of our race.

Take these friends of ours who used to attend early-morning Mass every day in a church in our old neighborhood. I lived but a short sprint away from the church, making it very convenient to roll out of bed, throw a long coat over my sweats, and heave myself into a cold pew. On the two or three occasions a year that I did this, I would see them there: sitting neatly in a row, dressed in Sunday best, in a pew that radiated warmth born of a long-term relationship.

Now that's a family worthy of an introduction to the cardiac surgeon.

I asked them once how they did it, and they just stood there, looking competent and embarrassed. I think one of them mumbled something about a "schedule." I was going to look it up, but I couldn't find the dictionary. Weeks later it turned up in a foxhole in one of the girls' rooms.

Oh well, I'm too busy to look it up anyway. Besides, I prefer triage. Why live under the tyranny of a schedule when you can just as easily keep up appearances?

If friends such as the family just mentioned drop by (which they rarely do because it's not on the schedule), it is best to focus on the point of entry. Do not attack the guests. Attack the clutter. In our house the point of entry also has a clutter target painted on it. It is the dining room, which is usually piled high with workbooks, school projects, and children. Before special occasions, add sewing to the heap. Once a week, Greg shuffles through the bills. During months containing the letter Q, we actually eat there.

Eating is another area where triage comes in handy. You see, the urge to eat strikes individual family members at random throughout the course of a given day. However, it peaks about two hours after supper, as soon as the last congealed blop has been wiped from the table, the last pasty crumb swept from the floor, the last greasy pot rinsed and removed from the empty, gleaming sink. This is the moment when a nameless man who lives in our house gets the urge to unshell a bag of peanuts. He is not really hungry. He just hates to see the table looking so bare and useless. Thinking purely scholastically, he sees that it needs a few thousand peanut shells all over it to fulfill its final cause.

And in a way I see his point. A kitchen table is built to serve for eating, so use it thusly. We homeschool mothers, too, are built to serve. We stand at the ready. So what if our tables be cluttered or our personal appearance fractured? What are our day's activities for, if they're not steps toward fulfilling our final cause as homeschoolers and homemakers?

Speaking of homemaking, if you are thinking of dropping by, give me a twenty-minute warning. If you don't, I may need the services of a cardiac surgeon.

∞

Sentenced to Hard Labor

Giving birth is getting easier these days. Once I discovered the epidural about four kids ago, that was it for the travail. I don't understand women who forgo this wonder of modern medicine. "Oh, I'd miss the drama," one told me. You want drama? Hang on. There is enough of that in raising a child to make up for weaseling out of the punishment of Eve.

Take, for one random example, teaching English. Being a writer, I thought this was going to be a breeze. It was, in fact, the real reason I homeschooled: so I could pass on my knowledge to my children. We started with phonics, and went through an indefinite period sounding like Fred Flintstone: "Ya ba da ba doo!" At first it was like early labor. Not too painful yet — but tiring. No fear! Once you get past that early stage, you're clear to get hooked up to a workbook. That's like the epidural. Your kid reads the directions; you lie back and relax a bit and let nature take its course. I recommend Catholic workbooks; that way your kid's English gets born and baptized all in one shot. For instance, Penmanship Grade 1:

Piety
Fortitude

Bless Me, Father, for I Have Kids

Martyrdom
Modesty
Beach
Attire
Should
Never
Be
Worn
To
Church
Hell
Damnation

Then composition hits, and it starts to get tough. The transition phase has begun.

Now, as each one of my daughters comes of age and gets ready to deliver her first paragraph, I get excited. What will it look like? Will it take after my stuff — short with clear features? Or will it resemble my husband's — long, serious, with a noble brow? At first it usually just looks like the stuff the other kids produced at this age — a red blob.

Unlike real birth, the smaller the child, the more labor-intensive the process. I keep forgetting this part. You know how time passes and you block out the pain? All you remember is the joy of having brought a paragraph into the world. That's good, because delivery gets harder with age. I don't have the stamina and flexibility I had when I taught the first three girls. Then again, I'm mellower. My expectations are not as firm as they once were, and my patience has stretch marks.

I've always deemed it best to begin labor on a Monday, after a couple of days' rest. Fasting is not recommended. Just the opposite, in fact. This time I have fortified my nerves with a piece of last night's chocolate cake. My fourth-grader is ready for the ordeal. It being her first time, she's not sure what to expect. So far, she's chosen her topic and made some random notes. I sit down beside her and get ready to coach.

Coach: Good job on the notes. Now we are going to organize them. Breathe deeply, relax, and think of a topic sentence. You want to introduce the reader to the idea that your favorite view is the Bridal Veil at Niagara Falls.

The child is willing, but wants this to go as quickly as possible.

Child: How about, "The Bridal Veil makes me think of the Blessed Mother trailing down like diamonds upon the rocks. The End"?

This is the sort of answer you get if you give an impressionable child a workbook containing about thirty million references to Catholicism. She thinks that if she dies trying to write a paragraph, she will at least go to heaven.

Not without passing through purgatory first, honey.

Coach: Hmmm . . . First of all, the Blessed Mother isn't trailing down — Niagara Falls is. Second, you don't want to use a detail like "diamonds" just yet. The details are for the middle sentences. You only want to introduce the idea that it's your favorite. Something like, "The Bridal Veil at Niagara Falls is my favorite view." Now you say it's your favorite, in a different way.

Child: Oh. "The Fall of the Bridal Veil at Niagara Falls . . ."

Coach: Stop. No. Its name is "The Bridal Veil at Niagara Falls."

Bless Me, Father, for I Have Kids

Child: The Bridal Veil Fall at Niagara Falls is the most wonder-fullest and beautifullest . . .

Coach: Hon, it's not a fall. It's a falls. Fall-z!

Slowly I begin to perceive the pain. I'm getting cranky.

Coach: This is not difficult! All you need to begin is . . . Here, I'll write it down: "The Bridal Veil at Niagara Falls . . ."

Enter Distraction One.

D 1: Mom! Do I have to write, "I will not interrupt" a hundred times?

Coach: No, but you can write, "I will not distract the little kids when they're learning something new" 1,200 times. Speaking of 1,200, how many times have we been over this?

Exit Distraction One swiftly.

Coach: Tell you what: forget the falls for now. Let's focus on saying it's your favorite in a different way. Think of how you can say it's your favorite.

Child: How about, "It reminds me of the horn on a unicorn's mane"?

I sigh, count backward from ten, take shallow panting breaths.

Coach: Right now we just need something general. This is what I mean, something like: "The world holds many beauties, but the loveliest of all is . . ."

Child: That's great! Let's use that!

Coach: No, dear. You think of one.

Child: I can't! You took it!

Coach: Dear, there are fifty more ways. If someone put a gun to my head, I could list them all. (*Did I just say* gun? *Violent thoughts are creeping in. Not good. But so far the only action I've taken is to grit my teeth.*)

Enter Distraction Two, grinning.

D 2: Hey, Mom. Why don't you just do it like you did with me?

Distraction Two demonstrates by grabbing Child around the neck and pretending to strangle. Child fights back and pulls Distraction Two's sweater.

D 2: Mom! She's ruining my sweater!

Coach: What do expect her to do? You grabbed her around the neck!

D 2: All I did was . . .

Distraction Two gently places hands loosely about Child's neck, as if swaddling a newborn baby.

Coach: (*to self*) Should I wait, or get the forceps now?

D 2: I just came in to get my math book. (*Exits.*)

Coach: Now, where were we? Oh yes, the first sentence.

Child: Niagara Falls has the most beautifullest and the most wonderfullest fall in the world, the Bridal Veil Fall.

Coach: Well . . .

Child: What's wrong with that?!

Coach: You're getting there . . . (*How do you break it to a kid that her sentence needs surgery? Best to be direct.*) There are no such words as *beautifullest* or *wonderfullest*.

Child: I've heard people use them before.

Coach: How old were they, five?

Child: (*nods*) Uh huh!

Coach: It's "most beautiful, most wonderful." Just take my word for it. But you're on the right track. Now, I'll make it easy for you. We'll keep, "Niagara Falls has the blank blank, but the most beautiful of all is the Bridal Veil." Now you just think of something to put in the blank.

Child: Most beautiful?

Coach: No, because you can't say that twice in the same sentence. Think of something else that describes Niagara Falls.

Child: (*Stumped silence.*)

Coach: Remember when we went there?

Child: Yes.

Coach: Well, what's the first thing you noticed? (*Unconsciously I sit up tall and hold my breath.*)

The Distraction Duo peeks in. Child sits and stares ahead. The Distraction Duo stands in front of her and begins making sweeping gestures describing hugeness.

Child: Vast?

The Distraction Duo burst into applause.

The logical thing to do here would be to quit while ahead, but I've decided I want twins. It should take only a couple of minutes, right?

Coach: Good! Let's try another one. Have lots of people heard of Niagara Falls?

Child: Yes.

Coach: That makes them . . .

Child: Popular?

Coach: Yeah . . . But people all over the world have heard of them, so they are . . .

Child: Worldwide popular?

Coach: Not exactly. It starts with an *F*.

Child: What's the next letter?

The Distraction Duo start imitating tourists, taking pictures and buying postcards. Child looks confused.

Coach: Famous! Tell you what. Let's just write, "Niagara Falls is vast and famous, but the loveliest part of all is the little Bridal Veil Falls."

Child: I'll take it! Quick, what is it again before I forget?

After only a half-hour of hard labor, a bouncing baby topic sentence was delivered. It looks a lot like me, which I guess is no surprise. I carried it for her. But that's okay. With a little more coaching, in a few years she'll have plenty of her own.

∞

Co-oping for CHICKENs

I'll finally admit it: the real reason I homeschool is fear. I am afraid to send my kids to school because of what might befall them. Namely, they might come home one day with a slip of paper that says: *Reminder: Items for St. Poormouth's bake sale are due next week.* Schools are too demanding. Even with tuition and bingo, they never have enough for basic upkeep like heat, electricity, and frog dissection. They keep going back to the parents. "We just need enough for a few state-of-the-art electron microscopes." Today you're selling Rice Krispie Treats; tomorrow you're out extorting pledges from relatives, friends, and neighbors for a spell-a-thon.

I thought I could avoid it all by homeschooling. And for many years I did. No matter how much work it was to teach my own children, it was easier than the endless stream of fundraising with which schools hold you hostage.

Then came the year my energy was so low I wanted to rename my homeschool "Armageddon Academy." That's when my friend Stephanie convinced me to join her co-op. CHICKEN (Christian Homeschoolers In Cooperation for Kids Education Now) was founded by evangelical homeschoolers but was soon flooded with Catholics. We had our own group, FISH (Forming and Inspiring through Schooling at Home), but it was just a social club; meetings were held almost by accident. CHICKEN was more organized; it offered actual classes. None of us wanted to quit homeschooling; we just wanted somebody else to do it for us. A once-a-week co-op was the perfect compromise. They'd teach our children things that we couldn't, and lighten our loads.

One of the courses CHICKEN offered was called "Life Skills: The Life You Save May Be Your Own." I had been unable to teach certain domestic skills to our eldest — such as using a can opener. She told me she was planning to be rich and have her own cook.

I leveled with her. "Latin was canceled, and the only other course available is Prom Planning for Puritans." No dancing allowed. She gave in.

The syllabus promised to cover balancing a checkbook, renting an apartment, and calculating interest and amortization on a loan. Grown-up stuff that appealed to her.

But when a cooking assignment popped up midway through the year, she rolled her eyes.

"An assignment is an assignment," I told her. (Ah, back up! Another reason I joined the co-op.)

"All right. I'll do it tonight. Let's just get this over with."

I grinned. A night off! This would be great. All I had to do was sign a slip of paper saying she did it.

Oh yes: and eat it.

Once she committed to the project, she cast me out. Now and then the banging of pots and pans would get my curiosity up, and I'd surreptitiously peek in. "Stay out! I want to do this on my own!"

A few minutes later she reeled me back in: "Mom, there's no food in this house!"

Technically it was not true. There was not *no* food. There was one stuck egg (stuck in its carton), a packet of two-year-old Kashi, and *plenty* of oats. However, I conceded, the Pringles had long run out.

"I think you were supposed to plan and shop . . ." I said.

She threw up her hands as if to say, "What next?"

Together we did manage to locate a box of pasta lurking under some ancient Tetley tea in the pantry. There were also various un-dated leftovers in the back of the fridge. I shuddered and floated out again.

An hour later she brought me the paper to sign. "Well," she said with a note of pride in her accomplishment, "that's a relief."

I glanced over at the pots on the stove. "The assignment says, 'Must include appetizer, main dish, side dish, beverage, and dessert.' Mind if I take a look?"

LE MENU

Entrée:
Elbow macaroni con sauce de can

Accompaniment:
Frozen veggies à la microwave

Beverage:
Aqua naturale de la faucet

Dessert:
La leftover cake from somebody's birthday

A bold achievement. I hated to mention it but: "I'm not seeing the appetizer."

"That's the frozen veggies, Mom! Kill two birds with one stone. Or, speaking of dead birds, we can count the chicken."

"What chicken?"

"I found a chicken leg in the back of the fridge and threw it in the sauce. There wasn't that much. We can say that's the appetizer."

Seemed perfectly reasonable. I signed the paper.

So the co-op wasn't teaching my child much in the way of cooking skills. But it was still lightening my load. Until one Sunday night when my second daughter handed me a note: *Reminder: Next week is your family's turn to contribute baked goods to the CHICKEN Co-op's weekly snack sale.*

"Is this what I think it is?" I exclaimed. "A fundraiser?"

"We have one every week," she explained matter-of-factly. "It's our turn. CHICKEN is trying to raise money for BAWK."

"BAWK?"

"Yeah, our drama club, Brilliant Acting With Kids. We charge fifty cents for each item. By the way, I forgot to give you the note last week . . . We need the stuff tomorrow."

I glanced at the clock. Ten p.m. Just a few short hours until morning, when I'd have to come up with the goods. I turned the note over. It was unsigned. It may as well have been written with blocks of letters cut out from magazines. I clutched my head.

"It's okay, Mom," said my daughter, patting me on the head (which had fallen out of my hands and onto the table). "I'll take care of it."

I squinted up at her. Of course! Why didn't I think of that? I was speaking to Sara Lee — the one who loves to bake.

Good old Sara enlisted the other two teens to help. After that, it was only a matter of finding a recipe that used ingredients we happened to have in the house. I heard the three of them discussing it.

"Chocolate chips? Nope. Somebody broke into them. There are only three left in the bag."

"Ah — muffin mix. Makes six. Not enough to go around."

"Cinnamon-roll mix — yes!"

"No! They have to rise for an hour. Do you want to be up past midnight?"

Finally, after excavating, the can of oats was discovered. "Oatmeal cookies! Hmmm. Generic oats. No recipe on the can."

"No problem. Somewhere in one of these five recipe books there's bound to be a recipe."

"Not this one — needs to chill for an hour."

"This one? No, we don't have toffee."

"How about this? Needs butter-flavor Crisco. We only have plain."

"Oh — let's just substitute!"

Halfway through the mixing, somebody called, "Mom, do we have corn syrup?"

"Why would we have something that you only eat as the second ingredient of breakfast cereal?" I answered. "Wait — one of my cookbooks has a page of substitutions. Where's that cookbook Dad got me for Christmas, *Crisis Cooking*? Here it is." *Flip, flip, flip.* "Carcinogens, Fats, Freezer Burns, Maiming, Poisoning, Salmonella, Spoilage . . . Ah hah! Substitutions: One and a half cups of corn syrup equals one cup sugar and a half-cup water."

"We need only a half-cup of corn syrup."

Luckily the kids take math at the co-op — and so they've learned the first principle of mathematics: grab a calculator.

"Cut one and a half to a half by dividing by a third. Divide one cup sugar by a third, that by a third, then one-half by a one-third by multiplying. That's one-sixth."

"Mom, there's no one-third measure on the cup."

"Wait, my cookbook has conversions. I saw it as I flipped past 'carcinogens.' Sixteen tablespoons in a cup, so one-sixth times sixteen should do it. That's two and four-sixths or two and two-thirds tablespoons of water plus the one-third cup of sugar."

Ten minutes later the kids peered into the oven. "Why aren't they baking? They're still just sitting there!"

Finally they came out of the oven, looking, in the words of one teen, "like little balls of poo."

"I won't bring those things and humiliate myself!" Sara Lee declared.

"We have to!" fought back another. "People bring in gross things all the time, and *they* still go."

"Yeah, it looks like somebody *went* all right."

"Once somebody brought those pink Rice Krispie things. I bought some."

"Oh yeah . . . So did I. And one time there was that chocolate-chip marshmallow-ball thing with animal crackers sticking out in a bag. I bought that because it had chocolate chips in it."

"Ew! Those things looked like they were in somebody's drawer for three months."

"I was desperate. It was Lent."

With two more weeks until Easter, that settled it. We wrapped the cookies up by twos in plastic, tied it with a red curly ribbon and labeled each one – Oatmeal Drop Cookies. We thought the name suited them.

Next year I'm encouraging all my Catholic friends to join CHICKEN. If we band together, maybe we can get some BINGO going.

∞

Homeschool Unceasingly

People sometimes ask me if I homeschool year-round. They figure, hey, you've got the teacher, you've got the students, you've got the location. Why drag yourself to the pool or to the playground in the summer? You can have a peachy time poring over workbooks.

Okay, it's not entirely unsound thinking. In fact, it's somewhat syllogistic:

If a) homeschooling is a commitment,

And b) homeschooling is an institution,

Then c) homeschooling is a commitment to an institution.

Right. If d) *you are insane*.

Still, I don't blame people for thinking this way. They're trying to picture homeschooling, and they're stuck on the only model they know: the classroom. They're rather like Hollywood directors who, sixty-plus years after *The Bells of St. Mary's*, still use the same costume to portray nuns — in pairs.

Let's see, according to this picture, we should have one large blackboard, one overhead projector, and several assorted classroom-size pets: goldfish, salamanders, and possibly a tarantula. For decor we have various instructional posters, such as an ABC scroll and the periodic table of elements, as well as a tapeworm floating in a jar of formaldehyde.

A bell goes off at 8:30 a.m., at which time all normal family activities cease — activities such as smearing cream cheese on a bagel, talking with your mouth full, grabbing the cream-cheese knife out of the baby's mouth. Students then file in punctually for the raising of the flag (you will need a cathedral ceiling) and the Pledge of Allegiance. School commences.

Each student (in uniform) sits at a little desk, while mother walks slowly down the row in those orange nylons that nuns used to wear. When he wants to speak, a student must raise his hand, even if he's the only one in the class. (If he gets the answer wrong, he snickers and whispers "duh" to himself. If he gets it right, he secretly envies himself and hits himself in the back of the head with a spitball.)

If it were really like this, I wouldn't blame the neighbors for calling in an exorcist.

It is common, however, for new homeschoolers to exhibit strong classroom tendencies. In the early years, I myself once went into raptures over a ten-inch plastic skeleton. It was perfect for gross anatomy. I had to have it! My normally zealous husband shook his head. How ridiculous! Our child was only in kindergarten. She would not be ready for gross anatomy until at least third or fourth grade.

In those days we had energy; we had creativity; we had no idea what we were doing. These days I sometimes meet a young, gung-ho mother who reminds me eerily of my former self — like this woman who was so eager at the start of homeschooling that she did it all of the time. I don't just mean year-round. I mean literally *all of the time*. We'll call her Dottie, because she was.

Dottie served alphabet cereal for breakfast and made her kids spell three words before they could take the first bite. At lunch

Homeschooling: The Early Years

Homeschooling: A Few Kids Later

Dottie had them do experiments with their food, such as seeing if ketchup freezes at the same rate as mustard. At dinnertime they set the table in German: "*Die Gabel*, the fork, *Das Messer*, the knife . . . Darling, you forgot *Der Loeffel. Wir* cannot *sippen die Zuppe*, without *der Loeffel.*"

Dottie's efforts didn't stop at home. At parties, too, she would commit random acts of homeschooling. Once she pulled her preschooler out of the sandbox and said, "Darling, can you find Mommy a sphere?" The child sighed and ran off. A few minutes later she returned, holding a can of beer. "No, sweetie," Dottie explained patiently, "that's a *cylinder*. Try again." The child sighed and ran off once more.

That gave a veteran homeschooler sitting nearby an idea. She pulled aside her preschooler and said, "Darling, can you find Mommy a beer?"

But Dottie's friends were concerned. It was one thing if Dottie wanted to self-destruct. It was another to tempt her kids to do her in. They tried to warn her: Earth to Dottie: it's called *home*schooling. This term does not apply to anyone's home but your own.

Dottie didn't listen. Her motto was: "Homeschool unceasingly. Sleep not. You should be awake praying that there will not be a test." Besides, she was too busy telling her friends about the new tapeworm she'd ordered online. Her friends wondered: what did Dottie's husband think? They thought he'd have stepped in by now. "What's in the package, kids? The mailman delivered a . . . what? Don't just stand there gagging. Mommy's gone insane! Run for help!"

Soon Dottie's friends lost track of her — on purpose. They wouldn't follow, and they couldn't keep up. However, they wish her well. Perhaps, they mused, eventually Dottie will learn to balance home and school. Even now she might be eating a box of Tastykakes in her pajamas while her kids watch a spelling video.

Or perhaps she has just learned to channel her original enthusiasm. Like most of us, maybe she has found there's no need to wear ourselves out inventing learning opportunities; the kids will do that. They have a native wide-eyed curiosity about the world around them. All we mothers have to do is support, encourage, and, at times, suppress it:

- What happens when you swallow a penny? Do copper plants grow in your stomach?

- How long does it take for muffled crying and the words, "Shh, okay, I'm sorry. Shut up! Sorry, okay? SHHH!" to travel from an accident scene to Mom's ears?

- How much climbing can a glass-topped coffee table stand before it cracks? Find out whodunnit when we dust for fingerprints.

- Explore the art of abstract mural painting with indelible markers.

- Use blunt-nosed scissors to create the latest in hip hair designs.

- Learn how to fold, crumple, and tear statements from the electric, gas, and water companies, thereby saving your family hundreds of dollars.

The patron saint of this type of activity has to be Thomas Edison's mother. We all know the story. Day after day Thomas Edison sat bored in Chalkdust Land, tapping his fingers in Morse Code, looking out the window, and never guessing he would someday aid and abet this scenario by inventing the electric lightbulb. Neither did the teacher who called him "addled."

"Oh yeah?" Mrs. Edison is reported to have said. "Just because he tried to hatch the breakfast eggs by sitting on them or burned down our barn is no reason to call my son an idiot!" *I know what I'll do*, she thought. *I'll teach him myself. Oh sure, I'll have days when I'll want to call him an idiot, but I can always tell him to go play with his train and telegraph set. By the time he gets back a few months later, I'll be refreshed and ready to begin again.*

All homeschoolers want our children to retain their most precious gift: that wide-eyed wonder they had when they were two. That never changes. When that happens indeed, they will be homeschooling unceasingly. Like Edison's mother, all we have to do is get out of their way and give them space. That way, when they burn down the barn, nobody gets hurt.

∞

Of Birds and Bees

Catholic parents, let me take this moment to commend you. When it comes to education in . . . well, you know, the, ahem, facts of life, you have bravely stood up for parental rights. You have said, "These delicate matters are for parents to attend to! No one must usurp this right! It is a solemn duty that comes from above." Papal documents in hand, you have prevailed!

I congratulate you, brave parents. You did it. You won this battle not just for yourselves but for all of us. I have you to thank for preserving my God-given right to discuss certain unmentionables with my children. Thanks a lot.

By the way, do you think you could help me out? I'm a bit overdue on the little talk, and I figured that you, being brave and smart and all . . . you could just fill in for me. I know — it's my job. Okay, you could pretend you're me. I won't tell. I'll let you wear my clothes. There's a new dress in the closet I've never even worn. You can return it even, if you'd rather have the cash. Here, use the car. Heck, why don't I just *give* you the car? You've earned it. I know, you take the car and drive my kids out to some remote location and explain it to them. As soon as they crawl back out from under the seats, bring them back.

Bless Me, Father, for I Have Kids

The fact is, I come from a long line of cowards. Don't ask me how cowards like my Yankee ancestors produced long lines. They aren't generally believed capable of it. But I'm here as living proof that they did manage.

Funny how inhibited societies are so fertile and this present one — in which trampy supermarket magazines are top sellers — is so sterile. It doesn't make sense. Did you see those ladies who were part of the polygamy compound? Necklines up to their chins, sleeves down to their knuckles — seventeen children apiece. The cover girl on *Cosmopolitan* owns a cat.

Anyway, my ancestors left me nothing to go on. There are no words I can repeat as heard from my mother, and her mother before. Oh, my mom *tried* to have the talk with me. In her mind I'm sure she succeeded. That's the flip side of being a Yankee. You do what you have to do and like it (which is probably where the long lines came from).

So she told me in very straightforward language, which is best for such occasions, "Don't sit on boys' laps." "Why?" I asked innocently, a mere child of seventeen. "Well, er . . ." she went on. "Boys, when they reach a certain age . . . want to . . . become fathers."

This struck me as very odd. I tested the information on guys I knew in high school. Take Keg Barnacle, the guy passed out at his desk in study hall. Was he in fact dreaming about pushing a small child on the swings? How about Thug Simpleton, the guy peeling out of the school parking lot in his beat-up Camaro. Was this a ruse? Did he nurture a secret desire to own a wood-paneled station wagon?

I didn't get it. But when the time came, it didn't stop me from dutifully bringing children into the world. Children who are now coming of age. Oh, don't remind me.

Of Birds and Bees

Well, I guess they could always fall back on the time-tested methods that made our country great: bad companions, PG-13 movies, and billboards advertising beer. Hey, it was good enough for me. Yet, my conscience tells me that the gutter alone is not sufficient. No, I need something spiritual. Something that teaches the kids the truth, beauty, and meaning of all this sort of thing. Hey! How about a book? Books have been the tried-and-true method of copping out for decades. I mean, why else do you teach kids to read but to get out of having to talk to them about this stuff? Lots of respectable parents rely on books.

Wait a minute, I forgot. In the immortal words of a respectable parent who once bravely won for me the right to not shirk my sacred duty: "Books are indecent." Oh.

Somewhere out there, there must be *some* book that can aid me in my duty. One to which even really strict parents would grant an imprimatur. In it there would be several pages devoted to birds, bees, and flowers. None involving kegs and station wagons. It would have things like birds flying low and flapping, grass seed resting on a bare hillside, and flowers demurely dying on the stem. Pictures, however, would be verboten. Everything presented would be sacred and pure and could be observed going on in one's own backyard in broad daylight, under parental supervision, of course. Binoculars recommended.

I could give such a book to my children without reserve and rest assured that soon they'd know all there is to know about botany.

But, alas, no such book exists to date. So perhaps I should just do my duty and write such a book myself: *The Devout Coward's Guide to Never Mind What.*

Thus equipped, I have every confidence that they'd figure out the rest of it. After all, their ancestors did.

∞

Phobias of the Small and Numerous

No matter how hard I try, it's impossible to raise children completely free of phobias. Fear is an effect of Original Sin, along with sickness, death, ignorance, weakness of the will, and inclination to hangups.

Our three-year-old has already survived one of our family's early-childhood phobias: a fear of public toilets, a.k.a. *McPhobia*. Her fear was not based on the usual reasons: that hundreds of people use them daily and that the wads of paper littering the floor are older than she is. It's that once a McDonald's handicapped toilet attacked her.

Not yet fully potty-trained, she had approached this vast receptacle at eye level. But with the trust of St. Peter when he first walked on water, she allowed me to hoist her onto the thing, and held on tight. Suddenly the automatic flusher went off like a giant sea-sucking squid. She panicked like Peter. I held her tight: "I am with ye, O ye of little faith!" Now that she survived that encounter, she has determined to rise above it. Whenever we enter a public bathroom, she points a commanding finger at the slumbering monster and yells, "Doan fwush!"

The next phase the shy kids in our family went through was *hello-phobia*. When people came over, they'd study the cracks in the floor tiles. I don't know what they were thinking. Possibly: "If I say hello, will my aunt bite me?" Perhaps I should have done more to show them there was nothing to be afraid of, like sniffing the person's hand, patting them on the head, and saying, "Friend."

That phase soon gave way. It gave way to the fears that come with adolescence. Top of the list is *frumpophobia*: fear of being seen in a skirt when every other teen at the party, except the statue of Mary, will be in jeans. It gets worse if your dad thinks it would be lovely to wear not only the skirt but a veil as well.

Around the same time, I discovered that some teen phobias are good. Girls fear being dropped in on when the house is dirty or when their hair is not done. This is a significant step in growing up. It means you can trust them to make the right choices. They no longer, for instance, suffer from *sudsophobia* — as they did when they were two and you tried to give them a bath. They'd scream for all the neighborhood to hear as if you were binding them with chains (an older child holding them still) and dumping boiling oil on their heads (warm bath water and shampoo). That's all in the past. Now they have a fear of letting the body develop its natural oils for more than twenty-four hours.

Clean and tidy is a double-edged pumice stone — like the kid who began her biology-class report: "I picked this spider because it is not as gross as the others." Luckily we do have one who does not gross out easily. (Every family needs at least one child who will stomp spiders and show stinkbugs the door when Dad isn't home.) She was born with more mettle than the others. She was the only one, for instance, who watched the cat giving birth. (The grossbugokid took one glance and announced that she was never getting married.)

This kid handles all the tough jobs — like making phone calls. The older girls are still in therapy to overcome their *phonophobia*.

Phobias of the Small and Numerous

Recently they broke through and learned to call Nana. In early youth they had been traumatized by the phone after I'd asked one of them to redial Nana, forgetting — horrors — that the last call had been to the arts-and-crafts store instead.

Like getting a wrong number, all children likewise share a fear of getting the wrong answer. The main symptom of this phobia is "upspeak." Upspeak was first discovered by a priest friend of ours who teaches religion at a high school nearby, and it signifies that tendency for the voice's inflection to go up at the end of a word, thus making what is technically supposed to be an answer sound like a question.

Father claims he can tell homeschooled kids because they don't suffer from upspeak. For instance, you ask one his name and he doesn't say, "Um, Jayden Albers*nagel?*" He puts a period on the end: "Isaac Jogues *Cal*laghan, Father."

Never mind that there are other ways you can tell . . .

I hate to break it to him, but all of our homeschoolers have suffered from upspeak at different times. It is usually brought on by math. It doesn't last, but when it strikes — around age ten — it is acute. The most obvious symptom is bluffing.

Me: How do you know which function to apply to this word problem?

Kid: Um, we studied it?

Me: No, I mean how do you know you should add here in this particular problem?

Kid: . . . Because otherwise . . . it'd be wrong?

This fear does have its beneficial side. A fear of getting the wrong answer can be channeled into academic hard work.

In fact, I'd go so far as to say that all fears are like that. The tricky part of parenting is determining which part of the fear to suppress and which to encourage. Every fear can be either good or bad, depending on what you make of it. I know all about these things because each and every one of my own phobias made me the confident, well-adjusted person I am today. I'm sure of it. At least, I think so. Well, if um . . . 'cause otherwise, how would I know?

Taking Home Education on the Road

Just when you think that homeschooling will save you from problems regular parents go through (such as having to buy a $2,000 wardrobe every August), the time comes when you have to take your life in your hands and teach your kids how to drive.

You've spent years running them to jobs, parties, classes, extra-curriculars, and holy acts of service. And frankly, you're sick of it. You're sick of waiting for them in parking lots while trying to think up constructive things to do while stuck in the car: such as reading your car owner's manual, perusing your insurance info, and adding up the digits on your driver's license.

When Miss Firstborn (MFB) was invited to a prom . . . about fifty miles away . . . that let out at midnight . . . that was it. She needed to learn to drive.

To save the 250 bucks that driver-ed professionals charge, Greg offered to teach her. I was skeptical. This is the guy who needs two weeks' notice to mow the lawn. Still, he felt sure he could squeeze her in between six and six thirty a.m. Wednesdays and every third Sunday afternoon in months ending with y.

Three months later, his cumulative total hours behind the wheel with this kid equaled about half a Rosary. I know this because it's about all I got through before they returned home and each started yelling at me. According to each of them, the other person was impossible and it was all my fault. Do not insist that they drive together again.

So I decided to teach her. What the heck? I potty-trained her, taught her to read, and to write "I will not choke my sister because she took the pencil I sharpened yesterday" a thousand times.

If there was anyone who can handle this job, I thought, it is *moi*. I broke the plan down to seven easy lessons.

Lesson 1: Do not argue with the instructor
This takes place in the driveway.

Me: Why are you sitting on your foot?

MFB: I can't see.

Me: Move your seat up.

MFB: It's up as far as it can go. This car is too low. We should get rid of it.

Me: You can't drive sitting on your foot.

MFB: I have to!

Me: It's not allowed.

MFB: Mom, do you want me to drive blind like little old ladies who can't see over the dash?

Me: Little old ladies do it.

MFB: They're a menace!

Me: Okay, then get a telephone book and sit on that.

MFB: Why do I have to do that? I'm at the perfect height right now. My leg works fine.

Me: Except for one thing.

MFB: What?

Me: I'm not giving you the keys until you put your leg down.

Lesson 2: Getting started
This takes place in the driveway.

MFB: (*Buckles seatbelt. Adjusts mirror. Checks lipstick*) What do I do now?

Me: Turn the car on.

MFB: Oh. I always forget that.

Lesson 3: Knowing your right from your left
This takes place in the driveway.
This should have taken place years ago.

Me: Okay, turn right out of the driveway.

Miss Firstborn moves fingers surreptitiously in the air over the wheel.

Me: What are you doing?

MFB: I can't help it. Playing the air piano is always how I distinguish my right from my left.

Me: Aargh!

MFB: But don't worry. I'm also wearing a ring on my left hand. (*Pauses. Moves fingers surreptitiously.*) That helps.

Lesson 4: Knowing who gets the right of way
This takes place out in traffic. Ye gads!

MFB: Is it my turn or theirs?

Me: Theirs. Wait for them to pass before turning.

MFB: How do you know it's theirs?

Me: You have a solid green and you are going left, crossing traffic. They are going straight.

MFB: What if I'm going right?

Me: Then you can just go.

MFB: What if I'm going straight?

Me: You go.

MFB: HOW CAN YOU TELL THEM ALL APART?

Me: If you are crossing traffic, you yield, unless you have an arrow.

MFB: What if I have an arrow and they have an arrow at the same time?

Me: They won't.

She ponders for a moment how I could know this mysterious truth. She looks at me, not sure whether to doubt or to worship me.

MFB: This is ridiculous. They should just have special cars that always get the right of way. You go get your license, and they tell you that you just get the right of way all the time.

Me: How would the other drivers know?

MFB: They could put it on your license plate. Or better yet, just paint the car blue. That's it. All blue cars get the right of way. And there are only two car colors allowed. Blue and white. White has to yield.

Me: What if two blue cars come to the intersection at the same time?

MFB: Oh.

Me: I know . . . (*I can't resist.*) You could have secondary colors. Blue and red yields to blue and yellow.

MFB: Yeah . . . but then what if two blue and red ones come at the same time . . .

Me: That's good homeschool logic. You're starting to catch on now.

MFB: Well it's still gotta be easier than figuring out who gets the right of way!

Lesson 5: Gas-brake dyslexia
This takes place in a store parking lot
after I pick her and her sister up from work.

Me: Pull into this parking spot and ease to a stop.

Car: VROOM!

Sister in Back: Aaaah! Please don't make me drive with her again, Mom. It's inhumane! I can't take it anymore! Please, please, please . . .

Me: How do you think I feel? She's only the *first*. After her it's you and five more besides. I'm popping gray hairs right and left. (*I point.*) That's *this* way and *that* way for *some* people.

Lesson 6: Home safe

Me: Now pull slowly onto the parking pad. Good.

MFB: Let's see — lights off, windows up, radio out, wipers off. Is there anything else? (*Begins to exit car.*)

Me: Put it in park!

MFB: Oh. I always forget to do that.

Lesson 7: Call a professional driving instructor
This takes place in a darkened room, lying down with your head on the yellow pages, accompanied by aroma therapy and soft music.

∞

Get on Your Knees and
Thank the Lord You're on Your Feet

"Catholic, eh?"

∞

Gimme, Gimme — That Thing Called Prayer

Growing up a cradle Catholic means that on top of begging your parents to get what you want, you pray for it. "O God, I want a new bike . . . Please let Dad say we can get a dog . . . Make Buck Testosterman move to Greenland so that he can't shove me off the swings anymore. Or if that is asking too much, please kill him."

The older I got, the higher I reached. Forget murder — in high school I prayed, "Let me get good grades." One time, when I got a C on a research paper, my prayers were answered. My teacher said so. Under the grade was a note: "Face it, kid; this is a gift." Seeing as I'd written the paper the night before, I was relieved I hadn't flunked. But really, lady, if you were in a giving mood, couldn't you have been a little more generous?

Still, it taught me to be more specific next time. So, at the beginning of my sophomore year, I prayed, "O God, this year let me pass *with flying colors*." Figured it beat studying.

That prayer came true, too. That was the year I joined the marching band.

It took many more years for me to understand the Catholic concept of *ora et labora*: Pray *and* work. Up until that point I had only heard of the Protestant Work Ethic and thought that meant Catholics should just expect miracles. Just one of the many strange and wonderful things that set Catholics apart from people of normal religions.

Speaking of strange religions, it could have been worse. I could have been born into a bizarre sect that required making cold calls.

Still, being Catholic has its fair share of embarrassing moments. Like when the kids have to put on a play or a piano recital in a Protestant church. They always try to genuflect. They're not looking for the red light. So what if there are cushions on the pews instead of kneelers? What does that mean? It's got stained-glass windows, and a table front and center. Green felt banners . . . Not to mention row upon row of pews. A young child sees all of that, and down he goes. That's okay. Until an older kid yanks him up and stage-whispers, "There's no Jesus in here!" You shrug at the old lady behind you, who happens to be the minister. How do you explain? It's automatic.

Kids also genuflect at the movies At least it's dark in there. They can pretend they dropped something. "Oh, sorry for holding up the line. No, I'm not making the Sign of the Cross. I *wasn't*! I had an itch on my head, and it traveled to my shoulders. 'Scuse me, mister, would you mind getting your feet off my pew?"

Or take saying Hail Marys. When I was small, my mother taught me to say a Hail Mary whenever I heard an ambulance. It's really a beautiful habit, and *habit* is the word; I don't know how many people I've prayed for whose car alarm went off. Now Greg and I have passed it on to our kids — who dutifully say Hail Marys when a siren goes off in a movie.

Being Catholic skews your cultural references, too. Once at a loud ballroom dance hall, I called my husband "Greggie" — my date name for him. And our ballroom teacher stopped me. "Did you just call him 'Reggae'?" "Oh no," I laughed. " 'Greggie,' like *Greg*orian chant. You know." He didn't know.

You probably don't want to tell these people that we also talk to the dead, keep their bodies on display, and even parade them around on special occasions.

I know we seem weird to everybody else. But we used to be mainstream; really we're just doing things the way Catholics have done them for centuries. Take holidays. The word comes from "holy day." In Catholic European countries, major feast days are postal holidays. That's fine over there, but here nobody in America gets it. In our homeschool, for instance, we never take Martin Luther King's birthday off. We can't — we already took Epiphany. But the neighbor kids don't know. They're at the door every twenty minutes: *Pound, pound, pound!* "Come on out; we have the day off!"

"O God, please let the neighbors move to Greenland. Or if that's asking too much . . ."

But you can't ask God to kill people. No matter how sorely you're tempted. Catholics are supposed to be nice, right? Turn the other cheek. The meek shall inherit the earth. "O Mother meek and mild, please kill . . . no, just kidding."

Sometimes this can cause interior tension. Like when you're out with your big family and somebody says to your face (and in front of your children, all of whom have ears): "Seven kids! Are you *nuts?*"

What's funny is, the people who call you nuts really expect you to act sane, and not like this:

"Nuts? Children, would one of you be a good girl and get the gun out of Mommy's diaper bag?"

No, that's out of the question. You have to just stand there meekly and try to stammer out something edifying. Or at the very least pray for the guy.

Hey . . . there's an idea!

Looselips' Fink Trips

After your kids have spent several years in formation in your home, you can feel confident about sending them out two by two to tell all the world the dirt about you. Things that you'd never publish in a book except for the fact that none of them are true.

We have one child who has shown herself creative with family lore ever since she was little, when she told a room full of visiting friends that Greg rolled over every night, put his arm around me, and said, "I love you, dear." And that I reportedly responded with, "Get out of here and go to sleep."

But I couldn't get mad at her. She who sins not with her mouth has perfect parents. Besides, from knee-high this child has possessed the divine gifts of big-heartedness, openness, and friendliness. Children always elected her leader of their games. Puppies clamored around her ankles. Kittens followed her home. Adults were enchanted with her big blue eyes, welcoming smile, and ready embrace — at which time she might say, "I don't understand . . . I can get my arms all the way around my daddy, but I can't get them all the way around you."

Yes, those were the Years of Speaking Dangerously. But by the time she reached her teens, I thought those years were behind us.

Then we sent her and her older sister to Germany to stay with friends for a month.

Greg and I thought it was a good opportunity for her to sharpen her language skills and experience our Old World heritage. Her older sister would go along to keep her and the family reputation in one piece. (If you can manage it, you ought to try to have both kinds of children: one type ensures entrance to all the fun life has to offer. The other makes sure you don't get thrown out.)

Living in someone else's household for a month, naturally you are going to swap stories. They tell you their views on spanking, and you tell them, if you are Fraulein Looselippen, your family's views on biting.

"In our house, when we bite each other, it's like the worst thing. It's worse than spitting."

Frau Hostess: *O meine gute!*

Big Sister, the Voice of Reason: We don't bite each other!

Fraulein Looselippen: Yuh huh!

They are both correct. The facts are that we do indeed bite each other. *We* are usually about two years old when we do it. *We* are then sternly corrected. So sternly that *we* apparently never forget it.

Or this one while visiting the ancient city of Trier, arguably Germany's finest example of Pax Romana, where St. Helena spent her old age in prayer and good works.

Voice of Reason: This is my dad's favorite city. It's where he spent his Fulbright year.

Looselippen: Yeah, didn't he get drunk here?

Reason: Uh, I never heard *that* one!

What else did she tell them — that we *had* to get married?

This is what comes of our little bedtime chats. At a certain age, I stopped telling bedtime stories and started telling them about the neat things that had happened to us in our youth.

For example, one evening I told the kids how their dad and I picked up a hitchhiker under some high-tension wires in the middle of a thunderstorm, and he took us to meet the Amish who were laboring past midnight to prepare a farm and craft fair. Another time I told them how we got stranded once ourselves and had to hitchhike when I was six months pregnant. At no time did I tell them we hitchhiked in the middle of a thunderstorm when I was six months pregnant, that I went into early labor, panicked, and climbed a high-tension wire, and was later rescued by the Amish and taken to their farm, where they applied their craft to heal me.

In bedtime-story fashion, she must have fallen asleep and dreamed the rest.

Perhaps this is really my fault. I should have brought her up the way I was. My mom had me pegged as a blabbermouth, so she gave me the mushroom treatment — kept me in the dark and fed me, er, fertilizer.

As the youngest of a family that came of age in the Sixties, I was lucky not to have been a particularly observant child. Starting when I was about six, all kinds of things having to do with friends, hitchhikers, drinking, and not being married began going on around me, yet I never had a clue.

But Mom wasn't taking any chances. One day she took me aside, lowered her head, and looked at me the way a bull looks at a matador and said, "Don't tell your friends about Jane's hip."

Bless my little heart, but it had never occurred to me that my sister Jane's being born with a displaced hip, which was fixed about eight years before I was born, was something to hush up. Still, this was as good as a commandment from on high. One that I immediately broke, because it had instantly begun burning a hole in my gossip gland. I picked out my most discreet neighbor and spilled the goods.

And then she told two friends, and so on . . .

Jane was too busy hanging around with friends who weren't getting married to notice. But I see now that Mom was training me, because when I was sixteen she took me aside, shut the door, and told me the *real* family secrets: which you couldn't pry out of me now with money.

Although . . . how much have you got? No, never mind. They're not all that bad anyway. I mean, nobody *actually* died.

Anyway, it's too late. I've told most of them to my children. Not the way Mom told them to me, but as they came up, naturally, so as not to seem too shocking.

And now look at the mess I'm in!

The only recourse, as I see it, is to handle Fraulein Looselippen the mafia way. Get something on her and threaten to spread it around. And at this age, there's one sure thing kids are too embarrassed to talk about.

I know who she likes! Na na na na na!

∞

Salvation by Scales

There is no more demanding occupation than parenthood. Few people would disagree with that. Okay, a vocal minority does hold that logging on the frozen lakes of Siberia is one; others argue that climbing high-tension wires in the middle of a thunderstorm is another.

Sure, sure. But have these whiners ever attended a piano recital? Definition: 1) a semiannual event lasting anywhere from two to five hours; 2) an event that spontaneously occurs at homeschool events throughout the year.

Such events are preceded by months of practice time, for which there is no known indulgence. Normally I am able to bear it, but when my energy is low, and I hear the hammering of scales, the safest place for me is the furthest corner of the basement laundry room. As I take flight, the strains of "You're Never Fully Dressed Without a Smile" are nipping at my very heels. "Tomorrow" is sure to be next. Whew! A close call.

This is the hidden life of many parents. Their untold story is one of dedication, selflessness, and heroism in the face of "Chopsticks."

Perhaps you are considering having your children learn piano. You imagine a warmly lit parlor, perhaps a few guests are gathered around, while your eight-year-old plays Beethoven's soothing, hypnotizing "Pathétique." Yes, I was once like you.

I imagined it would be like going straight to heaven. I forgot that practice makes purgatory.

As my family grew, I found out that in households with many children, the rate of piano-practice purgatory is exponentially higher than in average-size households. So I've come up with a handy equation to help parents project the number of hours they will spend in bondage to scales before reaching the pearly keys.

Add up the number of children you have, multiply that by the number of times per year a recital is likely to occur, then multiply that figure times pie — which you will be expected to bake and bring to the social hour afterward. To that number add the hours spent practicing, times the number of your children, times your STL (scales tolerance level). The equation looks like this:

$$H = C ® p/y):\text{-}P + C (PT) = J$$

Now I wasn't always this cynical. Early on, I couldn't wait for my child's first piano recital.

Nowadays I can always tell who the first-timers are by their enthusiasm. Take Mr. and Mrs. Clef. They arrive early and grab a front seat. (Those of us veteran piano sitters who also have toddlers to control prefer to sit in the lobby or possibly the car.) Mr. Clef sets up a tripod and camcorder in the aisle. Mrs. Clef nervously checks the battery on her digital camera. She uses the warmup time to take some stills of her child playing scales. These are for Grandma, who, after raising five pianists of her own, has excused herself this evening, citing a nerve condition.

When the performance begins, these parents pay careful attention to the program, ticking off the songs as each child goes up to play:

Moonlight Sonata for the Right Hand
Brandenberg Boogie No. 3 in G Major

And if this is a Christmas concert, expect such classics as:

Walking in a Boogie Wonderland

You see, before you get to Beethoven's "Pathétique," it is first necessary to master the student arrangements in the *Snoozboogie* series by U. R. Yawning. No problem. There are only about twelve books in the series. With diligent practice, this should take only six years.

Meanwhile a pair of select students announce each song, reading aloud from the program for the benefit of illiterate members of the audience. "Next we have Iwana Faint playing 'It Came Upon a Midnight Boogie.'" Iwana rises from her chair stiffly, her face red and her head down. Can't you just tell how psyched up she is?

Iwana's parents rise slowly from a prone position and rub their eyes. Iwana has been playing for about three years, so they're veteran recital nappers. They smile mildly as they listen, and do not wince when she makes a mistake, because they've heard them all before. By now the mistakes sound like part of the piece.

Back to the Clefs. When eight-year-old Treble is announced, Mr. Clef bolts out of his seat to operate the camera in the aisle. Mrs. Clef raises the digital camera over her head. "Sorry to block your view," she gushes to the people behind her. "Our son is about to play 'Eine Kleine Nachtboogie'!"

Behind her are the Faints. "That's quite all right," they respond, then roll over and wad the program up under their heads.

The Faints suspect that the Clefs have just returned home from a two-month cruise, during which time Treble was at Grandma's house playing that same song fifteen times a day.

Meanwhile I simply offer it up. Piano recitals — along with anchoring oneself into a stone cell, hairshirts, and hopping on one foot across a bed of pointy nails — are a time-honored way of gaining a plenary indulgence, provided we hold no attachment to murdering the piano teacher.

Redemption is at hand finally when it is our child's turn to play. Our whole family sits up on the edge of our pew. No matter how many times we go through it, there is something exhilarating in the moment.

I am never prouder of the girls' abilities than now. It can't be easy to play in front of others. They have chosen the better part, knowing that such experiences will aid them to musical excellence. With so many recitals under their hairshirts, they are mastering skills in an art that they can enjoy for the rest of their lives.

Then one day in the recesses of my laundry room, passionate strains of music come flooding through the walls. Real music. The kind that a child plays when no one else is around. I pause, forgetting all that came before, all that was necessary to get to this moment. I close my eyes and listen in a trance of ecstasy as my child fills the house with the glory of Beethoven.

Ah . . . Salvation!

∞

Slouching Toward Cuteness

My mother felt old for the first time the day I called her and Pop cute: "All my friends think you're cute."

I was a teenager. Cute was a compliment. Her response was, "Cute! Oh, isn't that great, Dick? We're *cute*."

Well, they *were*. They took evening walks holding hands. They played Scrabble together every night. They'd never had time to do those things earlier in their marriage. It was only in their mid-fifties, when I, the last of eight children, was old enough to button my own clothes, locate the cereal, and take myself to the bathroom — roughly age seventeen — that they could relax and indulge themselves in a few well-earned luxuries of retirement, such as root canal and orthopedic shoes.

That's when I first noticed they were "cute." Our daughter didn't wait so long.

We took her to the movies with us recently. It was our weekly date night, but at our age, neither of us had the urge to sit in the parked car and steam up the windows, so we invited her along. It was a late show (when you're old, that means nine p.m. — close to bed-time) on a chilly May night. I grabbed a pair of comfy socks and put them in my jacket pocket next to the tissues and pillbox full of Tums.

On the way, I phoned the children. "Put away the salad. You forgot last time, and it shriveled up." Meanwhile Greg cautioned me to leave the phone on in case there was an emergency at home.

"Oh, brother!" Our daughter burst out as we pulled up to the theater. "You guys are old!"

Old? She might as well have pronounced us legally dead. Whatever happened to cute?

Greg and I never thought we were old. After all, we still have very young children. That alone is supposed to make people guess we're at least ten years younger. And thank God we're healthy. In the Western world, people our age are supposedly in their prime.

Notice, I haven't mentioned what that age is. Suffice it to say that if today's advances in healthcare mean that fifty is the new thirty-five, then we're still traipsing carefree and gay through our late twenties.

I know, I know. My innocent use of the g-word above makes me sound eighty-five. And indeed there are some days I *feel* eighty-five (which by today's healthcare standards is the new seventy-four and a half).

I suppose I should count myself lucky that I'm still young enough to be in the Repair and Maintenance stage of life — the state when, if you get a few aches and pains, you simply get them fixed. The problem is that this coincides with the Broken Income stage of life. You never know how much these aches and pains are going to cost you to keep from reaching the age of the New Rigor Mortis.

One day, concerned about a toothache, I called my sister Mary Ellen. She's a nurse, so it is to her that I often turn for professional advice, reassurance, and compassion. By which I mean, *free* advice, reassurance, and compassion.

"What's the problem?" she asked.

"Hot, cold, and sweet. Plus I'm tasting metal. So I think my filling might be coming out."

"Is it a molar?"

"Yeah, you know those massive cavities I got when I was a kid? Day after day robbing [our brother] Andy's coin collection for candy. Then night after night faking out Mom by wetting my toothbrush. I think I'm getting my temporal punishment early."

"You might need root canal!" she exclaimed reassuringly.

(Professionals don't worry about causing people heart attacks.)

"Well . . ." I tried to be optimistic, "it could just be a loose filling. There's more metal there than tooth."

"You're over forty now. I had my first root canal when I was forty. Torture — the whole way."

"They didn't put you out? There's this dentist around here who advertises sedation dentistry."

"No, you just suffer through the whole thing. But after Dr. Goldmolar, you oughta be able to handle anything."

Dr. Goldmolar was an old-school dentist who was long on nose hair, long on ear hair, but short on patience. Don't look him up. His name has been cleverly changed to protect myself just in case he is still alive (118 is the new ninety-seven) and tries to come after me with his professional dinosaur pliers. He had plenty of patients — our whole Cavity Family — but no sympathy for kids who frittered away their brother's Indian-head nickels on candy and then ran their toothbrushes under water.

"Remember how he used to put one foot on the chair and lean on our faces to get leverage?" said my sister nostalgically. (He was gentler on his carpet. He made all the patients slip into paper shoes.)

"Yeah," I shuddered. "I hear the cracking of my permanent teeth being ripped out whenever there's lightning outside."

"You know it," she said. "And after that, the bloody gauze-filled crater."

"Is root canal worse than that?"

Mirthless professional snort.

"Thanks," I said. "My dentist, you know, he's the no-frills type. He's pulled baby teeth and filled cavities on the kids with no novocaine."

"You *will need* novocaine for this one. Trust me. If he doesn't give you novocaine, you're definitely going to bite him."

My palms were starting to drip. "I think I'd better hang up now . . . I don't think this conversation is good for me."

"Wait . . . did you say you're on antibiotics for a sinus infection?"

"Yeah."

"That's good. Because if it's an abscess, it'll keep the mercury toxicity level down."

"It could just be a loose filling . . ."

"Doubt it." And she hung up, no doubt thinking, "Another satisfied customer!"

I guess I had it coming to me. For years I'd been torturing my other sister Jane about her health. We look a lot alike, so whenever she complained about some ailment, I would grip her arm and say with the compassion of Mother Teresa, "Did you have that when you were *my* age?"

I knew if Jane survived it, I probably would, too. Then again, if she had developed the dreaded disease later on, I, too, was probably fated to get it. Over the years, I have seen this come true on every level except pregnancy, which I have heard is not caused by genetic inclination alone.

So before calling the dentist, I called Jane. "Did you have this when you were my age?" I asked with alarm.

"When I was your age," she said, "I had insurance."

So much for my theory. I did not get the dental-coverage gene. I did, however, get the tooth fixed. It *was* only a crack. I lay back in the dentist's comfortable recliner while he pried the prehistoric filling off my molar, suctioned out a lung, and then replaced the filling. It took only an hour with the plastic mouth stretcher ironing my lips back against my face. When it was over, I could have sworn he asked the assistant if she had used starch to get such fine creases.

But I didn't care. I don't care even now that the tooth is still sensitive to hot and cold and I can't chew jello on it. I avoided root canal!

That and all the other breakdowns that come with old age make me glad we no longer have the life expectancy of, say, Noah.

Now, people have told me this is morbid talk — mainly my children. Children do not relate to death. Perhaps it's fear. Not for themselves, because they are too far removed from death. Their lives are just beginning. They fear it for their parents.

Our oldest child remembers us when we were young and hip — when Greg wrestled with the kids and I chased them around the yard. Nowadays we usually let the older kids do that sort of work, while we sit and enjoy the show. Much like our middle-aged cat, sometimes we get that old urgency to chase something, but ordinarily we're just happy to laze in the sun and lick our fur.

That's how I remember my parents when I was little. They were already middle-aged. I never experienced them as they appeared in home movies: Pop building a sledding hill in the winter and digging a swimming hole in the summer for my many little (bigger) brothers; meanwhile my Mom seemed pregnant in perpetuity. That was all over with when I at last came along. The brothers built the sledding hill and later, their wives produced a standing army of kids. All the while I was still a child.

Greg and I are not grandparents yet, but middle age has begun. Oh, it's not that bad yet. He's still got plenty of hair, and I look hip enough when my hair is highlighted. In fact, people compliment us on how great we look for having a) so many kids and b) such big kids.

Some people tell me I look like a teenager myself, and could be my teens' older sister. These people are usually 103 years old and

"Noah insists he's not too old for this. He says 600 is the new 425."

wear their glasses hanging from a chain. But I'll take it. Older sister to these blossoming beauties . . . okay, way older sister . . . okay,
would you believe older sister who was found in a basket on the
doorstep and adopted when the parents were four?

Our oldest likes hearing me complimented even more than I do.
That's why she rebels when we act old. That night in the movie
theater, after Greg paid for the tickets (note: she didn't make noise
about that one), I hobbled after her. "Hold the tickets, dearie. My
hand is shaking, and I might drop them." She started walking
faster. "Wait for me . . . my legs don't go as fast as they used to."

She turned. "Mom, *stop* it."

"Just a minute, I need my extra socks. It's drafty in here."

"Mom, people are looking! Put those away, and please don't
make me sit next to Dad. He narrates."

"Okay, I'll sit with him. That way I can lean over and ask him
what they're saying."

"Dad, make her stop!"

"Eh?" He cupped his ear.

At that moment I flashed back to a similar night when my
lower siblings and I went to the movies with my folks. They were
in their late fifties, and we were grown. It was their wedding anni-
versary, and after eating out, we went to see *Ferris Bueller's Day Off*
— where we all guffawed until people's heads turned. Afterward
they excitedly told us about the grave plot they'd purchased. They
insisted we drive out with them to see it.

My dad looked at it scientifically. Death is inevitable and the
plot was a good price. My mom thought the spot was *just lovely*.
She tried in vain to get us to appreciate it. *We* just wanted to get
the holy hill out of there.

What was wrong with these two healthy, young-for-their-age
people?

Now that I have my own family, I realize what was going on. My folks weren't in any hurry to die, but they were past the denial stage. There was no sense to worrying about the inevitable. The only thing worrying gets you is wrinkles. Besides, they knew their grave plot was just a resting place. They were expecting to rise again.

∞

Planning Your Child's Dream Education

Preparing our eldest for college had stressed me out so much that one night I couldn't sleep, but lay awake fretting. What did I know? I was just a housewife. What talent did I have to prepare this child for her future? I was fresh out of creativity. And it wasn't as if I could go the store for more. What if there was a missing ingredient? The proof would be in the eating. After all those years of slow cooking, choosing the best ingredients, adding just enough spice but not too much, my timer was about to go off. My firstborn was ready to take her place in that great smorgasbord of higher education.

Which college was right for her? A cheap, anonymous, local school with an easy commute? An established Catholic university with established Catholic rules such as "All drunken orgies must cease by three a.m."? Or a brave, young, poor Catholic college dedicated to pondering man's perennial questions, such as: "How am I ever gonna pay this whopping school debt?"

Then there was the problem of getting in. Did she have the salt? Had I done enough with her? Why couldn't she just work for another year until her juices ran clear?

I jumped out of bed and for some inexplicable reason, went straight to the kitchen, talking to myself.

"Now I'm learning to be a guidance counselor!"

You're halfway there, said a voice just over the sink.

"Wha . . . ?"

You've taken her through a college-prep program, registered her for a state-accepted diploma, and sent her for SAT prep.

"Who said that? Come in, Orson."

Actually, here they call me Tom. (We're all one big, happy family.) But you know me as St. Thomas Aquinas.

"You sound just like that guy from 'Mork and Mindy.'"

Stop letting your imagination run wild! That's the problem with you.

"I can't help it. St. Tom, I'm exhausted."

So what else is new? That's the Christian life, Carissima. Actually, it shows you're on the right track.

"Do you always look on the bright side?"

It's hard not to from where I'm sitting.

"St. Tom, help me. We haven't even begun to apply. We're in the visiting phase now, but I just had a baby. So we're cruising the Internet from the comfort of my desk and taking virtual tours. There are thousands of schools! After this we have to narrow down our choices to the ones whose baseline SAT scores match the kid's. Meanwhile she has to finish high school. She got a second job. She's burned out, too. Neither of us has the strength even to fill out a simple application. Name, address, social-security number . . ."

Don't forget the essay.

"Essay?"

All colleges expect an essay; it's part of the application process.

"Oh yeah. What's it supposed to be about?"

It? Each college has its own essay. There is no "it."

"Well, they just want some personal information, right? Just a little getting-to-know-you exercise?"

Uh . . . try the High Schooler's Guide to the Galaxy. But in the case of a homeschooler it shouldn't be too hard. Homeschoolers are known for deep thoughts. Your daughter has bursts of inspiration, right?

"Well, last night after we finished the Rosary, she jumped to her feet and exclaimed, 'I have to go shopping!' "

Well, good . . . There must be some way you can channel that.

"She could write an essay on the effects of Original Sin — how, after giving Adam the apple, Eve was horrified to discover that she had nothing to wear."

Hmmm . . . maybe you should get a book that tells how to write a college essay.

"Yeah, I've seen those at the bookstore. *How to Get into College for the Rarely Sober.*"

Not that one! I was talking about: I'm Not Only a Student, I'm Also Going to Be the President.

"Is that the one that features kids whose SAT scores look more like a tax return? I saw it. Not one of them left high school without a resume. Why don't these geniuses leave college to the dumb kids and do something really useful with their lives, like pay down the national debt?"

Some of them do. Did you notice this one?

Annie Warbucks writes about how being an orphan shaped her character. Using her Daddy's inheritance, she founded Annie Idol, a talent search for orphans. Her intended major is Perky Music Therapy.

There. It's not exactly Gregorian chant but it's a start.

"St. Tom, do you know how discouraging that story is? I suppose it's only fair to give our child the same chances we had, but look at Greg. You know, we ran into one of his professors from Big U. not long ago, and he never forgot Greg. Said he was the best student he ever had. He could speak Russian and German so well, he was offered a job with the CIA."

Yes . . . back in the Eighties. As I recall he didn't want to dodge bullets.

"So where is he now? Working for the Church — and you know what *that* pay scale looks like."

But we're taking note of it up here, and we have a great retirement package. By the way, you can pin it on St. Francis for steering him into Church work. (Cough.) You didn't hear that from me.

"Okay, then, look at me. I went to college, and I never did anything amazing. I became a housewife like my mom, who only had a high school education. What if our daughter ends up doing the same thing?

Ahem, let me think about that one . . .

Question: *Whether your child should go to college. We thus proceed to the first article:*

Obj. 1: *It would seem that your child should not go to college. She will be away from the bosom of the family.*
Obj. 2: *Further, she would rack up debt.*
Obj. 3: *She might smoke.*

On the contrary: *It is written, "O reason not the need! You heavens, give me that patience, patience I need. O Fool, I shall go mad!" Sorry for getting carried away . . . I've had several hundred years up here with Shakespeare, and he kinda rubs off on you.*

Anyway, I answer that: The real question is: Why did your parents send you to college?

Your parents knew that keeping you in the oven like an overdone soufflé would leave a bad taste in everyone's mouth. You were already puffed up and hard to handle. You needed to go somewhere and find out what you didn't know. That was the beginning.

Then there were your talents. Up here, certain Persons (I won't name Names, but They travel in Threes) are not too pleased with people who don't use them. College was where you found out you had some. So you smoked a little. With my help you didn't burn.

"I used to talk to you a lot back in those days. Did I ever say thank you?"

No, it was just: "Eek! Help me with my Latin. Help me with my paper. I need a miracle!" But it's okay, I'm the forgiving type. However, if you do feel a sense of obligation, then give your daughter the same chance. Have you ever thought about what it was that gave you the inspiration to homeschool her and the other half-dozen in the first place, Mrs. Just a Housewife? It was your education! I egged you on, of course.

"You did?"

Sure, me and Shakespeare and Dante and Plato and Augustine and Dostoyevsky. I hate to say it but even Hobbes, Locke, and Rousseau. Even Chaucer with his ribald tales. Remember how you read the one about Chanticleer the rooster to your kids because you thought it was G-rated? Hah! Lucky they were too young to follow it. We laughed a lot up here about that one.

It's your education that has kept you laughing too. It's your education that makes you dream these crazy dreams. Can you imagine what your dreams would be like if you'd never gotten to know me and my friends? You'd be dreaming about talking to Oprah right now!

It was indeed a scary thought — what might have been. Sure, I was no scholar like my husband. But I had feasted at the banquet prepared by my betters, and done what I could to keep the leftovers warm for my children. Learning together had been a treat for all of us.

"Thank you, St. Tom," I said. "You've cleared my head."

That's my specialty.

I started sleepily heading back to my room. *And don't worry about your daughter,* he called after me. *When I was her age, my family kidnapped me and locked me in a room with a strumpet to try to destroy my vocation, like some fraternity hazing prank. They called me an ox, but no one can call me dumb."*

"And I may call myself just a housewife," I smiled over my shoulder, "but I make great leftovers."

∞

The Samaritan Next Door
A Parable

Now it came to pass that Susie was a married woman, who was the daughter of Richard, the son of Amable (who took upon himself a new name as soon as he was of age, and that name was Mack), who worked from sunup to sundown, tilling the earth like his fathers before him. And her husband was Gregory, who, like his father before, was born with a telephone growing out of one ear. And he labored long throughout the day and sometimes into the night. He had not even sometimes a moment in which to eat his repast or lay his head upon his pillow. But often would fall asleep sitting up. And the snoring thereby would shaketh the house.

And Susie had lived with her husband now nineteen years. And this woman was impatient, waiting for the consolation of her husband. For their burdens were many. And many an evening she walked with him so that the ringing of the phone (which had been surgically detached) reached not his ears.

And Greg did spend his substance on their seven children. Susie did teach them at home, and their food she did cook with her own hands, and she oversaw the management of her home. And this she was glad to do, for the Lord hath given her strength like her father and mother before her, who worked from sunup to sundown, and the cabbages of the soil planted by her father, her mother did harvest and salt out the slugs thereof. Thus did Susie sing this canticle: Blessed be the Lord, the God who giveth joy to my youth and maketh me not to live upon a farm.

She made not herself a private chamber. For the upper part of the house was filled with children and the lower was filled with their stuff. Her chamber was like unto O'Hare Airport, the comings and goings of it being many. And it being used for the daily tasks: the swaddling of their firstborn son, the reading of the lessons, the surfing of the Internet: though there was nary a space to walk amongst the furniture. Much being the clutter found therein. And the young didst build Lego castles under her desk, and many a night she did dash her foot on the smaller pieces in the dark.

And unlike her husband, she did rarely fast from coffee or chocolate lest she become dangerous to the children. For she feared her own weakness.

On a certain evening, when they had lately finished their repast and the children were clearing the spaghetti pots, Susie spake unto her husband:

"Behold, the teenagers wax strong. Let us leave the children with them for a space and go up together and circle round the dwellings of our neighbors. For they have but recently planted flowers and the air is lovely this evening."

And they went up. And they took not the cell phone. Neither did Greg stop in the office to check his messages. For Susie was sore fatigued, and they had not reasoned together in many days. And Susie longed to make complaint to him of the doctor's receptionist who lately had made her inscribe herself in the file as "unemployed."

While passing by the dwelling of a certain neighbor, it happened that they spoke and made his acquaintance. And this man's

name was Anas (friendliness), for he was a foreigner, being but recently come into this country.

Upon hearing that they had seven children, Anas was truly
amazed. And he wondered aloud if Greg was rich. And when Greg
replied "nay," he was exceeding stunned. Then he wondered aloud
if Susie did work outside the home. And when she replied "nay,"
his eyes did open and he was passing dumbfounded. After a space
he did find his tongue and then he said to her, "So you do nothing?
You just watch the kids all day?"

And the demon did tempt Susie to wrath.

But she remembered the law of hospitality taught to her by her
mothers before, which read: "Do not give your neighbor a cabbage
with a slug in it." And she did not make to place her mighty hands
on the door posts and shake the house down. Instead these words
she spake in her heart: "I will not curse this place. No, I will bless it.
Because the things said therein are not from malice but ignorance."

And Greg replied kindly to Anas and explained all that must
be done during the day. Of himself, too, he spoke, and made the
man to understand. And the man offered wine and coffee. Then
he, opening his mouth further asked, "How old are you guys?" And
he did turn again to Susie and remarked, "You look so young to
have seven children."

And Susie was exceeding gratified. Now, this man was a Samaritan.

And they divulged to him their ages — which were but half
the years of Susie's grandfather when he did forget he dwelled in the
senior home and escaped often to walk back to the farm, because
the senior homes in those days had not security systems.

Then they said, "Now it is time for us to depart. The children
will wonder where we are." And Greg did say to the man, "Besides, I must do my taxes and Susie must attend to the housework,
for it is late and we will surely be up past midnight."And they bade

him farewell. And the man said, "Come up again if you have time."

And this he meant truly, for he earnestly desired to make a friend of them. And Greg and Susie found much understanding in that place. And Greg and Susie were exceeding glad they stopped on the way and did not quicken their pace. Nor did they keep to themselves nor hide them behind the proverbial fence. For the Lord desired them to know the stranger, for the stranger was a man after His own heart. And they prayed He bless the house of Anas, and its children and its children's children unto the seventh generation.

∞

Our Father

Let's see . . . How do I get started? Our Father . . . Now what? Hallowed be . . . Sorry, I'm always so distracted.

You don't mind, do You, that I wait until the end of the day to pray? I try to pray during the day, but there's no alone time except in the shower. And even that gets interrupted. When the sound of running water reaches the kids' ears, they take it as a signal to bring up that major life choice that's been on their minds.

"Mom?"

"Gurgle-what-gurgle?"

"Can I fuzzy bluh bluh my gummy?"

"Gur-what?"

"Can I fuzzy bluh bluh my *gummy*?!"

I think for a second. "Yes" would certainly get rid of the child. Then again, what would I be saying yes to? What if Fuzzy's mother calls later from the ER and demands to know where I was when the gummy went off and bluh-bluhed all over Fuzzy?

Then again, "No" guarantees more such talk.

"Well, Daddy said to moo-moo fur nippo."

So *he's* sent them. That rules out, "Ask your father."

"Wait 'til I gurgle out, for heaven's sake!"

Now what was I telling You? It's hard to concentrate on a conversation when in the back of your head there's a little voice trying to tell you that you're wasting time just talking to someone. Not that we shouldn't talk. Just that my hands should be doing *something*. At least I could be delegating jobs to the kids.

You see, I'm trying to break my habit of multitasking. Right now the baby's teeth need brushing. Simple, right? Yeah, if I went into the bathroom to brush his teeth, I'd brush my own, too, and then start cleaning the sink. I'd be trying to talk to You with one hand in the baby's mouth, one hand on the sink, and a toothbrush sticking out of my mouth. You see how ridiculous it gets. So I am determined to ignore all of it until You and I are finished talking. Only one thing at a time. That's what I keep telling myself.

What's on my mind as I lie here at the end of the day is that I really need Your help. Sorry if I'm always asking for favors. You know our house, Sparrow's Nest? Lately, it looks more like The Don't Drop Inn. Just look around. In the dining room there's a clean load of unfolded laundry that's been sitting in the basket so long it will come out shaped like a square. Fish are gasping in their swamp tank, hoping that the Big Hand in the Sky will send new water. This morning I saw their lips moving in prayer. (By the way, what did they say?) The entryway has an unfinished paint job that's about to expire — one year from starting date. I hung the pictures up anyway. A couple of stray raggedy children wander aimlessly about. The toddler pulls out her fountainhead hairdo whenever I'm not looking. Now her head looks like a spoon handle is growing out of it. The baby throws handfuls of Cheerios on the floor, hoping he can go back to them later when he wants a snack. Afterward he tries to wash his hands in the toilet.

We *do* have a couple of fat, well-groomed cats. They thrive in ruins, I'm told.

It's not that I don't attend to these matters. Far from it. I attend to them all day — a little at a time. If I have to go into the dining room to clean up a crayon bomb (Spoonhandle's work), I grab an item of laundry as I walk by, fold it, and lay it on the table. True, I've just created another visual mess without even beginning to clean up the crayon fallout. But I *feel* as if I am making progress.

Thus I proceed all day, sampling each job as if I'm at a smorgasbord. But that's gonna change. *Only two jobs at a time.* That's my new motto.

My husband thinks I'm an *Überfrau* of efficiency. He can focus on only one job at a time. Lately he's been complaining that he never gets anything done. I try to cheer him on whenever he manages to get *one* thing done. One whole thing! That's more than I manage; I'm in fractions. But he tries to imitate me. When he fails to get even one thing done, he makes up for it by working nights.

That reminds me, who is this Todd guy? I know he's one of Your friends, but what does he think we are, a suicide hotline? I'm talking about the guy who called at midnight. I leapt out of bed like a gazelle and grabbed the phone before it woke the baby.

"Hello?"

The guy says, "Oh, excuse me, is this the office?"

I'm like, "Not unless I've died and gone to purgatory."

"Uh, my name is Todd, and I'm trying to reach your husband."

"He's unconscious at the moment," I told him, and added, "and if I can't have him, nobody can."

"Really? What time is it there?"

"12:30 a.m."

"Oh, I do apologize. I didn't know it was so late. It's only 11:30 here."

"That seems pretty late to me too," I said.

"Well, your husband said to call him anytime."

"Todd, that's a figure of speech."

"But he said, 'day or night.' "

"Okay, hold a minute and I'll put him on." I held the phone up to Greg's heavy breathing.

What does he think, Greg is like those saints who can bilocate? Sleeping soundly in their beds while at the same time absolving sinners on a battlefield hundreds of miles away. You and I both know he is more likely to be found slumped over the computer at three a.m., drooling into the keyboard.

Is that the phone ringing at this hour? Oh, where is it? Dear St. Anthony . . . Could You wake up St. Anthony? Sounds as if it's coming from under the couch cushions. No, I'd better not answer. You and I are talking. Then again, I was supposed to call somebody . . . Now who was it?

Maybe I should answer it. No. I'll call them back in a few days. I'm sticking to my motto: Only three things at a time.

Can You believe I used to get bored? When I was a kid, I'd go to my mom and whine, "I'm bored!" She'd always suggest cleaning something. Hmmm, I know where she was coming from.

Sometimes that little voice in the back of my head taunts me: "Mom got up early. She mopped regularly. She got a decent supper on the table every night."

"Little Voice, shut up."

But my little voice is right. Mom was just better than I am. You know: Depression, WW II, tough times, the Greatest Generation. (Sorry, I talk in sound bites these days.) What I mean is, she was born older. She was born responsible. Well, I don't have to tell You. You were her Best Friend.

My husband thinks I'm just like her. "You're just as capable as she was."

"But I am not!" I try telling him. "I'm a kid!"

It's weird, but I really don't know how I function as an adult. It's such a relief to go visit my father's house. Whenever I'm at Pop's, I sleep like a baby. He may be eighty and I may be all grown up, but he's in charge. My little voice says so. I am off the hook. I'm a guest. No, I'm better than a guest; I'm an heir. The fridge belongs to him, but I can open it and take whatever I want. His spare room is rent-free. He's even got a garden. Just go out and pick a fresh tomato. Best part, he's loaded and loves to take me out to dinner.

Hmmm, reminds me of You.

It's not that easy to fall asleep in my own home. I used to try falling asleep saying the Rosary. You know how St. Bernadette was said to fall asleep saying, "Mama, mama"? I like that idea. But it never worked. I kept myself awake trying too hard. It was *work*. In the middle of it, I'd get distracted thinking about what I had to do the next day.

Anyway, as I said when we talked last time, just help me do whatever I should be doing.

'Scuse me, but did You just say, "Then shut up and go to sleep?" I didn't know You talked that way.

But I'm not done yet. I was leading up to something. Oh, what was it, Little Voice? I get so scatterbrained. Was I worried about the kids? No, that wasn't it. Right now they're all under our roof. There's no better feeling than that! Was it Greg? No, he's all tucked in for the night at his desk downstairs. It must be something about me then. I need to do something, and I keep forgetting what it is.

?

Oh yes. I wanted to thank You.

Now goodnight, Daddy.

∞

About the Author

Susie Lloyd was born into a large Catholic family that spanned the baby boom through the hippie and preppie decades. She was educated in parochial and public schools and a parent-run catechetical center and is a graduate of Thomas More College of Liberal Arts. She has won two Catholic Press Association awards for her columns in *Faith and Family* and one for her humor book, *Please Don't Drink the Holy Water!* (Sophia Institute Press, 2004). She and Greg have been married for twenty years and have seven lively children. She writes from the middle bench of her full-size van.

∞

Sophia Institute Press®

Sophia Institute is a nonprofit institution that seeks to restore man's knowledge of eternal truth, including man's knowledge of his own nature, his relation to other persons, and his relation to God. Sophia Institute Press® serves this end in numerous ways: it publishes translations of foreign works to make them accessible for the first time to English-speaking readers; it brings out-of-print books back into print; and it publishes important new books that fulfill the ideals of Sophia Institute. These books afford readers a rich source of the enduring wisdom of mankind.

Sophia Institute Press® makes these high-quality books available to the general public by using advanced technology and by soliciting donations to subsidize its general publishing costs.

Your generosity can help Sophia Institute Press® to provide the public with editions of works containing the enduring wisdom of the ages. Please send your tax-deductible contribution to the address below. We welcome your questions, comments, and suggestions.

For your free catalog, call:
Toll-free: 1-800-888-9344

Sophia Institute Press®
Box 5284, Manchester, NH 03108
www.sophiainstitute.com

Sophia Institute® is a tax-exempt institution as defined by the Internal Revenue Code, Section 501(c)(3). Tax I.D. 22-2548708.